D0845847

ZigZag Pass

By Leon Hesser

Printed in the United States of America

Published by:
BHP
Bavender House Press
P.O. Box 770883
Naples, Florida 34107-0883

Tel: 239-254-1478
Fax: 239-234-6198

Publisher's Cataloging-in-Publication
Hesser, Leon F., 1925-
ZigZag Pass: love and war / Leon Hess. -- 1st ed.
p. cm.
Includes bibliographical references and index.
LCCN 2008926878
ISBN-13: 978-0-615-19852-1
ISBN-10: 0-615-19852-X

1. Hesser, Leon F., 1925- 2.World War, 1939-1945—Personal narratives, American. 3. World War, 1939-1945 --Campaigns—Philippines. 4. United States Army—Biography. I. Title.

D767.4.H66A3 2008   940.54'2599'092
QBI08-700058

ZigZag Pass

Also by Leon Hesser

The Man Who Fed the World: Nobel Peace Prize Laureate Norman Borlaug and His Battle to End World Hunger (hardback, 2006; trade paperback, 2008)

Nurture the Heart, Feed the World: The Inspiring Life Journeys of Two Vagabonds (2004)

The Taming of the Wilderness: Indiana's Transition from Indian Hunting Grounds to Hoosier Farmland: 1800 to 1875 (2002)

To Florence …

My lover, my inspiration, my companion, my wife …

For more than 60 years.

"Now to the infantry—the God-damned infantry, as they like to call themselves. I love the infantry because they are the underdogs. They are the mud-rain-frost-and-wind boys. They have no comforts, and they even learn to live without the necessities. And in the end they are the guys that wars can't be won without."

Ernie Pyle
May 2, 1943

Foreword

Leon Hesser's memoir is as much love story as it is war story.

We were three veterans of World War II, Leon, Jack Hild, and I, when we first met on the evening of November 10, 2006, more than 60 years after the war ended. We were a panel of three who sat before a class of students at Hodges University who were studying the literature of war. The professor of the class, Dr. Scott Kemp, had invited us to share some of our experiences as young soldiers and to respond to questions.

While each of us had served in different theaters of the war, I was especially impressed with many of the similarities, especially between those of Leon and me. I related to so much of his story. We were both teenage soldiers who had experienced and survived intense, bitter battles. And we agreed that the duty in foreign countries had served to stimulate our interest and curiosity about global issues. It stretched our minds beyond the relatively closed communities in which we had grown up.

Several months after we had met at Hodges University, Leon shared with me a draft of his memoir. He said it was stimulated by the experience that evening before Professor Kemp's class.

Leon's story is delightful. Several things about it impress me. One is the way he and some of his closest buddies in basic training at Camp Hood, Texas, in essence formed a surrogate family as a means of tempering the pain of being away from loved ones back home. Also significant is the positive influence that his exposure to new and different cultures in foreign countries—notably the Philippines and Japan—had on his professional career. The experience guided him toward helping to relieve poverty and hunger in poorer nations of the world, first in Pakistan at a time when the Asian subcontinent suffered pockets of starvation, and then in Washington, DC, as director of America's program of agricultural technical assistance for less developed countries of Asia, Latin America, and sub-Saharan Africa. And finally, Leon's subtle humor throughout his story demonstrates his ability to survive under adverse conditions and at the same time shows his knack for enjoying better times.

Intertwined throughout is a charming love story, including the romance of his returning home to Florence, the girl whom he met just three months before going to the Army, their wedding shortly after he turned 21, and their early married life as young Indiana farmers. When Leon turned 30, recognizing that he had regretted that he had not gone to college, Florence encouraged him to sell his farm business and enter Purdue University as a freshman. He says going to college was so much easier than farming that he stayed on and earned a Ph.D. in Agricultural Economics.

With encouragement from Leon while he was a graduate student, Florence became a freshman at Purdue at age 35 and ultimately earned a doctorate in education. She then served as professor and director of the Reading Center at The George Washington University in Washington, DC, for 20 years. Her career is at least as fascinating as Leon's.

This is a story for all ages, but will be especially inspiring to our country's young people. I heartily recommend it both as absorbing history and as an endearing love story.

Peter Thomas
April 15, 2008

Contents

Leon Hesser

Introduction

One can never completely squash the memories of war—the sound of whining and exploding shells, or the shrieking cries for medics, medics, medics, or the sight and the putrid stench of a friend's corpse that had been exposed for three days beneath the scorching tropical sun.

My horrid memories of ZigZag Pass and later, Mindanao, temporarily faded during the elation of celebrating the end of the war, the fascination of occupying Japan, and the excitement of returning home. The memories faded, yes, but they never disappeared.

This memoir chronicles my personal experiences as an initially indestructible, subsequently frightened, teenage soldier whose invincibility vanished on his first day in ZigZag Pass.

* * *

On November 10, 2005, the eve of Veterans' Day, I was a member of a three-person panel of veterans of World War II. The audience was the students in Professor Scott Kemp's class at International College (now Hodges University) in Naples, Florida, who were studying the literature of war. They wanted first-hand exposure with real-live survivors.

Jack Hild had served in the China-Burma-India (CBI) theatre as a member of the famed Flying Tigers. Peter Thomas had survived D-Day and the Battle of the Bulge in Europe. I represented the Pacific theater where, as a newly minted private in the U.S. Army's 34th Infantry Regiment, 24th Division, I participated in battles to liberate the Philippines. The three of us were impressed with the eagerness and sincerity of the college students to learn more about this "ancient history."

All three agreed that when we returned from the war, we did not want to talk about it, we did not want to think about it, we just wanted to get on with our lives. But after my experience with those young people—seeing how eager they were to learn about the various conflicts—I thought: *Maybe I really should write about my experiences, my thoughts, my anxieties, my fears, my dreams.* A few days later, during an early-morning walk in our village in sunny southwest Florida—with my four granddaughters in mind as audience—I

9

mentally outlined a memoir, and started writing. By telling the story, I hope to entice my granddaughters and their contemporaries, older teens and young adults, to seek more knowledge about this important period in history.

My approach is to provide an historical context, or overview, for my two-year experience in the Army, for which three days in ZigZag Pass—February 3, 4 and 5, 1945—were the apex. This was my baptism by fire. In those three days, within a week after I had joined the 34th as a new replacement, half as many of our troops were killed or wounded as were lost in the outfit's bloody 75-day Leyte campaign.

Writing this memoir has been hard. More than once, as I mentally revisited the horrible events of ZigZag Pass, including the losses of several buddies with whom I shared basic training at Camp Hood, Texas, I sobbed. In a real sense, though, writing the story has been therapeutic. It helped me bring into the open some of the angst and torment that I harbored, suppressed, for more than six decades.

Right after the worst experience of my life came the best. I had met and fallen in love with Florence, the girl of my dreams, a scant three months before I went to the Army. The hard part, of course, was our being apart for those two years. We married within two months after I returned home. She has put up with me for more than sixty years, now, and was the inspiration for my having a remarkable career.

The Battle of ZigZag Pass was the single most traumatic event of my life. The impact lingered. Over the years, I often asked myself, *Why was I spared when so many were not?* Perhaps my Camp Hood buddy, Brenton Hirsch, had the answer when he said to me many years later, "Somebody up there had plans for you."

I have reflected on that statement many times. Serving with the Army overseas opened my eyes to how other people live. Since I lived through it, it wasn't all bad. For me, and I would guess for many others, the "good" side of the war was my having observed the people and cultures in the Philippines and in Japan that differed markedly from those of the Midwestern United States in which I grew up. It gave me a broader perspective on life and its purpose, and it made me realize that not all people in the world are as fortunate as we are in America. It stimulated a yearning for me to do something to help people in poorer countries.

After we married, Florence and I farmed for several years.

Knowing that I regretted not having attended college, Florence, a city girl, convinced me to sell the farm business when I was 30 and enter Purdue University as a freshman. It was so much easier than farming that I stayed on and earned three degrees, culminating with a Ph.D. in Agricultural Economics.

Shortly afterward, I joined the U.S. Foreign Service. We were assigned to Pakistan where I was director of America's technical assistance to help increase food production in that hungry nation. I and my staff helped Norman Borlaug start what came to be known as The Green Revolution, which dramatically relieved hunger in India and Pakistan. For that, Dr. Borlaug was awarded the Nobel Peace Prize in 1970. Those were heady days.

In 1973, I transferred to a plush office in Department of State in Washington, DC, where I was director of America's worldwide effort to increase food production in poorer countries. After early retirement from the State Department, I consulted on agricultural development projects in some twenty countries of Asia, Africa, and the former Soviet Union.

But those experiences are the subject for another book. I mention them here simply to suggest that had I not gone to the Army, I would almost certainly have remained on the family farm in Indiana. However virtuous that would have been, it would not have left me with the tremendous sense of accomplishment that I received from putting more food on the tables of millions of the world's hungry people.

Without doubt, the time in the Philippines and Japan inspired me to want to see more of the world and to try to level the playing field. My playing a role in extending life-giving benefits—relieving hunger and poverty of the World's poorer people—has indeed been healing. It has been a gratifying counterbalance to the horrors of ZigZag Pass.

Leon Hesser

Chapter 1: Indiana Farm Boy

Where better to grow up during the Great Depression than on an Indiana farm, near the small town of Winchester, in the eastern part of the state. We didn't have much money, but neither did the neighbors or my school classmates, so we didn't know what we were missing. We always had plenty of good food to eat.

Not all children at the time were as fortunate as I. In 1939, the year that I started high school as a freshman, John Steinbeck's Pulitzer Prize winning novel, *The Grapes of Wrath*, was published. This was the story of an Oklahoma farm family that, during the Great Depression, lost their farm to a bank and was forced to seek work in California as migrant workers. Many other rural families also lost their farms and their livelihood.

That same year—1939—the whole world started to change. On September 1, the day that I started high school as a freshman, Hitler's Army invaded Poland. I learned about it during class on American history. The teacher was almost as naïve as we kids. When one of the students asked the teacher about the meaning of Hitler's action, the teacher said, "Yes, Germany is causing some problems in Poland. But, we are studying the history of our great country. Have you read your lesson?"

On September 3, Great Britain and France declared war on Germany. On the radio that same day, in a fireside chat, President Franklin Roosevelt declared the U.S. neutral in the European conflict.

My favorite high-school teacher, like most Americans at the time, agreed with the President's statement of neutrality. Mr. Beck said, "The war is Europe's problem. We Americans are perfectly safe, with the Atlantic Ocean on one side of us and the Pacific on the other. There is no way that an enemy could reach us to cause harm. Let the Europeans work out their own problems."

All during my freshman year, Hitler caused havoc in Europe. When a few German U-boats appeared off the eastern shores of the U.S., people started to worry a bit, but the sentiment was still very much against our going to war. Knowing those feelings, President Roosevelt stated, "I shall say it again and again and again. Your boys are not going to be sent into any foreign wars."[1]

About the time I started my sophomore year, the U.S. Congress decided it was best to be prepared in the unlikely event that, somehow, we were drawn into the conflict. Congress passed the selective service act in September 1940, creating the first peacetime draft. Men aged 20 to 36 were required to register. Initially, fewer than a million men were drafted. Each was to receive one year of training. As the conflict heated up in Europe, the length of training was extended, more men were called up, and the draft age was reduced to 18.

My parents didn't talk about it much, but I sensed that they were concerned that I would soon be 18 and be subject to the draft. They were also keenly aware that the U.S. was not prepared for war and, if America were drawn into the conflict, it would be a long drawn-out struggle.

Then, on Sunday, December 7, 1941, the unthinkable happened. As a 16-year-old junior in high school, I simply was incapable of comprehending the implications of the Japanese bombing of Pearl Harbor, America's military base in the Hawaiian Islands. The sunrise attack killed 2,390 Americans and injured 1,178. Most of the casualties, 1,177, were on the USS *Arizona*, which sank in less than nine minutes. Twelve ships sank and nine were heavily damaged. More than 320 U.S. aircraft were destroyed or heavily damaged.

Mr. Beck was as much in shock as I. Everyone at school, teachers as well as high-school students, buzzed about Pearl Harbor. Why had the Japanese done it? What did it all mean?

There was no longer any doubt about the U.S. position. On December 8, President Roosevelt made a speech before Congress:

Yesterday, December 7, 1941—a date which will live in infamy—the United States of America was suddenly and deliberately attacked by naval and air forces of the Empire of Japan.

The United States was at peace with that nation and, at the solicitation of Japan, was still in conversation with its government and its emperor looking toward the maintenance of peace in the Pacific. ... the distance of Hawaii from Japan makes it obvious that the attack was deliberately planned many days or even weeks ago. During the intervening time, the Japanese government has deliberately sought to deceive the United States by false statements and expressions of hope for continued peace. The attack yesterday on the Hawaiian islands has caused severe damage to American naval and military forces. I regret to tell you that very many American lives have been lost. In addition, American ships have been reported torpedoed on the high seas between San Francisco and Honolulu.

Yesterday, the Japanese government also launched an attack against Malaya.

Last night, Japanese forces attacked Hong Kong.

Last night, Japanese forces attacked Guam.

Last night, Japanese forces attacked the Philippine Islands.

Last night, the Japanese attacked Wake Island.

And this morning, the Japanese attacked Midway Island.

Japan has, therefore, undertaken a surprise offensive extending throughout the Pacific area. ... As commander in chief of the Army and Navy, I have directed that all measures be taken for our defense. But always will our whole nation remember the character of the onslaught against us.

No matter how long it may take us to overcome this premeditated invasion, the American people in their righteous might will win through to absolute victory. ...

With confidence in our armed forces, with the unbounding determination of our people, we will gain the inevitable triumph—so help us God.[2]

That same day, the U.S. Congress passed a declaration of war against Japan. "Remember Pearl Harbor" became the war cry. But the U.S. remained ill prepared for a major conflict.

On December 8, the next day after Pearl Harbor was bombed, in an hour-long assault at Clark Field and Nichols Field in the Philippines, Japan wrought catastrophic damage to U.S. aircraft.

On December 10, Japanese forces invaded Luzon, the northernmost island of the Philippines. Three weeks later, on January 2, Manila fell. General Douglas MacArthur's combined American-Filipino forces were poorly armed, had antiquated artillery and a miserable supply situation. MacArthur withdrew his troops to a defensive position on the Bataan peninsula, on the west side of Manila Bay. When the defense of Bataan became hopeless, by secret order of President Roosevelt, the General left for Australia on March 17 to establish a new headquarters as commander in chief, Southern Pacific.

As General MacArthur prepared to leave the Philippines he declared, "I shall return."

On April 9, Bataan fell to the Japanese after a heroic defense by a greatly outnumbered force. America had suffered the most devastating military defeat in its history. At dawn the next day, April 10, 1942, the Bataan Death March began. The outside world would not know until 21 months later that American and Philippine prisoners suffered unimaginably brutal treatment.

The first authoritative reports about the Death March were conveyed in April 1943. With the aid of Filipino guerrillas, three American officers escaped from the Japanese prison camp in Davao, Mindanao, to an American submarine that delivered them to Australia. At MacArthur's headquarters, they provided details about servicemen being starved, tortured, and executed in what came to be known as the Bataan Death March. In hopes that Red Cross aid would get to the remaining prisoners, the news was withheld. Finally, on January 27, 1944, to the horror of Americans, the information was disclosed.[3]

The American captives were forced to march 65 miles in six days, mostly through jungle, with but one meal of rice during the entire trek. Of the total of 12,000 Americans and 66,000 Filipinos who began the march, about 5,200 Americans died. Many more Filipinos perished.

On the Island of Luzon, nearly three years later, in the Battle of ZigZag Pass, a teenage Indiana farm boy would help avenge the atrocities of Bataan.

Life on the Farm

Meanwhile, growing up on an Indiana farm during the Great Depression was excellent preparation for the rigors of military training. I grew up within ten miles of where my ancestors had settled in the wilderness three and four generations earlier, in conservative east central Indiana. My earliest remembrance was living with my parents and sister, Vivian, a year younger than I, in a worked-over log house in the village of Lickskillet, a few miles from Winchester. Lickskillet consisted of Miranda's grocery; Miller's garage; a lightly-used church held over from the nineteenth century with two entrance doors in front—one for the men and one for the women; and a dozen houses within walking distance of the grocery store, which doubled as the town hall. Men in the neighborhood sat around the wood-burning stove each evening and swapped stories.

The Hesser house no longer looked as though it were basically a log structure. It had been built onto, weather-boarded and fitted with a porch and swing in front. The Rural Electrification Administration had not yet brought electricity to the area, so we had a kerosene cook stove and kerosene lamps. All the neighbors had the same, with one exception: the Merandas had a Delco generator that provided electric power for lights for both the grocery store and their home next door. But the gasoline pump in front of the grocery store was still manually powered by Gail Meranda's moving a long lever back and forth as he watched to see when the gasoline reached the intended gallon-marker on the cylindrical glass container. He would then stop pumping and, by gravity, empty the contents through a hose into the customer's car or truck. At 15 cents a gallon during the Great Depression, not many customers said, "Fill 'er up!"

In 1935, when I was ten, we moved to a fairly large farm that Dad had rented on a crop-share basis. Even before the move, Dad had taught me to drive the family's 1929 Oldsmobile. After the move, I drove the car twice a day, less than a mile each way, to feed the livestock at an alternate set of farm buildings. Dad bought a new 1935 Model A John Deere tractor which I drove to prepare land for planting corn and soybeans while Dad planted the crops with a horse-drawn planter. Dad bought a John Deere tractor because it had a hand clutch, which I could activate. Most other makes of tractor had foot clutches; I was not yet heavy enough to activate a foot clutch. Nor was I strong enough to raise and lower the two-row corn cultivators on the tractor, so Dad invested in an easy-to-manipulate hydraulic system.

Leon's Saturday Job in winter: Hauling Manure

I enjoyed working in the field, especially on the brand-new tractor. Dad spent much time with me, even before we moved to the new farm, teaching me how to care for the pigs, cows and chickens. At the new farm, Dad expanded the livestock holdings to include a stable of draft horses and a flock of sheep. There were plenty of chores to do. In those days, no one in rural areas ever thought about "child labor" in a negative way. Since pioneer days, farm boys were expected to share the workload from an early age.

Even after we moved to the new farm, we continued to attend the church in Lickskillet. Sunday School was held every Sunday morning. A self-ordained preacher held church services on alternate Sundays. On Easter Sunday and at the Christmas service, there might be as many as twenty in the congregation; most other times, fewer. When I was twelve, I was baptized by emersion in near-by White River. Although the stream was muddy from the spring rains, the process cleansed my soul of any lingering sins. (I had quit smoking when I was seven; I got caught smoking corn silks behind the barn.)

My Christian heritage stemmed mostly from my mother's side. Her parents were influenced heavily in their religious beliefs by Great Grandma Acenath Smith Edwards, who was born in the Indiana wilderness in 1838. I was seven when she died at age 94. She spoke in "thees" and "thous." She was a wonderful storyteller and frequently told me about her childhood days in the wilderness at mid-19th century.

I attended Lincoln School for twelve years, the same rural consolidated school from which my mother had graduated in 1919. There were fifteen in my graduating class; nine of us had been together all twelve years. The school term ended in late April, early enough that we students could help our fathers with spring planting.

Lincoln high school, class of 1943. Leon is 4th in front row

Lincoln had no gymnasium; we on the basketball team practiced during recess on a cinder-floored outdoor court. Twice a week, the team was transported by school bus to a real gym for practice. Even with this lack of facilities, we usually did well in competition with other county teams.

We had no electricity or running water on the farm until I was twelve years old. Our toilet was an outside privy. Being awakened before sun-up to do the morning chores was common, everyday routine.

By the time I was 16, production of food was crucial for the war effort. The U.S. was shipping tons and tons of grain and other foodstuffs to Europe in addition to supplying our own Army, Navy and Marines. Therefore, young men on farms with large acreages of crops and substantial herds of livestock were given draft deferments.

At the beginning of the war, my father's farm business consisted of 240 acres rented on a crop-share basis. We had eighteen dairy cows, a dozen sows whose pigs we fattened for market, a stable of draft horses, a flock of sheep, and Mother's poultry and egg operation. Mother traded her eggs for the bare essentials of groceries when the huckster made his rounds in the neighborhood once each week in a Model A Ford truck converted to a mobile grocery store.

Besides helping year-around with the livestock chores, my primary job in the spring was to drive the John Deere tractor pulling a disc harrow to prepare the land for planting. Dad followed with a team of horses pulling a two-row planter to plant corn or soybeans. Dad competed with neighbors to see who could plant the straightest rows, which always transited the fields in the direction that would make the longest possible rows.

When the crops started growing, I drove the tractor to cultivate the corn and soybeans, to keep pesky weeds under control.

The Battle Abroad

On April 18, 1942, when I was a junior in high school, Lieutenant Colonel Jimmy Doolittle secretly led a squadron of sixteen B-25 "Mitchell" two-engine bombers, each with a crew of five, in a daring operation that took off in the middle of the Pacific Ocean from the USS *Hornet*, an aircraft carrier especially modified to transport the bombers. Each plane carried 2,000 pounds of bombs and enough fuel to hit Japan and continue toward China. Most of the planes dropped their bombs on Tokyo; a few targeted Nagoya.

The Japanese high command was deeply embarrassed. As the nation's capital burned, Emperor Hirohito grew furious; how could American planes have reached us?

When the American press asked President Roosevelt where the planes had taken off from, he said, "From Shangri-La." The news of Doolittle's Raid was a great morale builder for Americans. Roosevelt promoted Doolittle to Brigadier General, and he was awarded the Medal of Honor.

To eliminate the risk of any more such raids, the Japanese resolved to destroy America's aircraft carriers. This led them to disaster in the four-day Battle of Midway—June 4 to 7, 1942—a decisive battle that marked the turning point in the war in the Pacific. The Japanese had planned to capture the U.S. strategic island of Midway, to use as an advance base. Their strategy was to entrap and destroy the U.S. Pacific fleet. Our intelligence had cracked enough of the Japanese code to learn that they were planning to invade Midway, in the middle of the Pacific Ocean. The analysts determined the exact date of the planned attack.

With brilliant tactics, the U.S. Navy organized its defenses and destroyed all four of the large Japanese aircraft carriers in the battle, the same ones that had attacked Pearl Harbor: the *Akagi,* the *Kaga,* the *Soryu,* and the *Hiryu.* The U.S. lost one carrier, the *Yorktown.* The Japanese lost twice as many planes in the Battle of Midway and suffered 3,500 deaths compared with 307 for the Americans.

During the battle, Japanese destroyers picked up three U.S. Navy aviators. After interrogating them, they murdered all three.

Soon after the Battle of Midway, the U.S. and its Allies took the offensive in the Pacific. News that the tide was turning caused me to want to become involved.

As soon as I turned eighteen, in the summer of 1943, I registered for the draft. The local draft board determined that I should be deferred; my services were needed to produce food. I had mixed feelings. My best friend, Wayne McGuire, had joined the Navy Air Corps—he really looked sharp in his dress blues. I was envious.

Wayne McGuire and girl friend, Alice Mae Green

In the fall of 1942, Dad bought his first 80 acres at a farm auction. In retrospect, the price, $91 per acre, was extremely reasonable. But at the time, when he had to borrow most of the money to finance it, it seemed to Dad like a fortune. To help cover the cost of the farm, he decided to have an auction sale. Except for a team of draft horses and four cows, he sold off the livestock in the fall of 1943. We now had 80 more acres to farm, but no longer had a large holding of livestock. At the same time, pressure to fill quotas in the spring of 1944 caused the local draft board to reclassify me to 1-A.

Edgar Billman, the owner of the 240 rented acres, pleaded with me to let him go to the draft board and ask for reconsideration: "You are really needed here on the farm; your father cannot handle it without you."

I did not consent. My best friend was in the Navy Air Corps; I also wanted to be a hero.

When I went to the Army, Dad sold the team of horses because he could not simultaneously drive both the tractor and the horses. Then, rather than plant corn in straight, parallel rows, he tied the two-row planter behind the disc harrow pulled by the tractor and planted 'round and 'round, ending up in the middle of each field. Neighbors teased him, but because of his ingenuity and putting in longer hours, he was able to keep the farm going.

After I returned from the service, Mother told me that Dad worried about me a lot. He would frequently have to stop the tractor in the middle of a field where he was cultivating corn. Thinking about where I was and what danger I might be in, with tears in his eyes, he could not see well enough to avoid uprooting the corn plants.

Boy Meets Girl

In March 1944, three months before I left for the Army, I met Florence Life. I had completed a three-month stint at the local glass factory in Winchester, Indiana. It was time for me to return to the farm to help Dad plant corn and soybeans. I was captivated by the combination of the sparkling, charming personality and good looks of the young lady in the personnel office who processed my termination-of-employment papers.

The following Saturday night, my high-school buddy Cliff and I went to Winchester's Rainbow restaurant, a prominent hang-out for young people. Florence and a friend were sitting in a booth next to the door, sipping Cokes. She smiled and said, "Hello, Leon. I'm Florence. May I introduce you to my friend Alice?"

I was charmed by her friendly manner, her warm personality, her genuine smile. Later, I mentioned that I was surprised that she had remembered my name. She said, "I not only knew your name, I knew your whole history!" from the personnel files at the office.

The next day, Sunday afternoon, Cliff and I went to the Rainbow to indulge in another Coke. Guess who? She was standing, this time, with her friend Melba. I judged her come-hither smile to be an invitation to chat and started edging in her direction when—oops—she dropped her handkerchief. (She swears to this day it was accidental.) Slightly embarrassed, I picked it up and with a half-grin handed it to her. The ensuing conversation led to a double date that night.

Gasoline was rationed: three gallons a week for non-essential driving. Cliff calculated that he had enough gas that he could drive the four of us in his 1934 Ford roadster to Union City, 10 miles to the east of Winchester, to see a movie. I don't remember much about the movie, but I still sense the blissful feeling of romance as Florence and I held hands. Her witty reaction to the movie's plot and characters and her charming persona caused me to think, *This is one swell gal.*

On the way back to Winchester, Florence and I sat in the back seat and held hands most of the way. The whiff of her freshly adorned makeup was intoxicating. As the only daughter in a prominent family, she displayed the polish of a sophisticated city girl. When Cliff stopped in front of the Life family's residence, I was impressed—overwhelmed—by the size of the house, with its giant pillars in front.

In my rural naiveté, when I took Florence to the door, I neither kissed her goodnight nor asked for another date. Big mistake! I had to call her six times before she agreed to a second date. We dated several times over the next few weeks.

Leon and Florence in love

Then, during May and early June, we were together often. We were in love. For me, it was love at first sight. It took a bit longer for Florence, who was undoubtedly influenced by a mother who had higher expectations for a son-in-law than a farm boy. I have always suspected that Mrs. Life was secretly pleased when greetings from Uncle Sam meant that I had to report for Army duty.

On June 6, four days before I was to report to Fort Benjamin Harrison, near Indianapolis, 150,000 young American soldiers stormed the beaches of Normandy, France. The chilling D-Day news—quickly circulated on the radio, local newspapers, and newsreels at movie theaters—was a stark send-off for this Indiana farm boy.

On June 10, my parents took me to the bus station in Dad's 1939 Ford for me to make the trip to Fort Ben. The night before, Florence and I made a commitment. She would wait for my return and I would win the war as quickly as possible.

Randolf County, Indiana, boys off to war. Leon is 4th in back row

Chapter 2: Basic Training at Camp Hood, Texas

When I arrived at Fort Ben, I was asked to fill out a form indicating which branch of the service I preferred. Again, thinking of my best friend who was in the Navy Air Corps, I checked "Navy." After standing in long lines to go through the induction procedures, I finally arrived at the desk of the man who would proclaim my destiny. "Mr. Hesser, you have requested the Navy, but the Navy quota is full, so you will take the Army. *Next man.*"

The Army measured and outfitted me with Army drabs, sent my civvies back home, and gave me the proverbial crew cut. Within two days, I was on a troop train headed for Camp Hood, Texas. During the two-day train ride, I learned that Camp Hood was in the "beautiful hill and lake country" deep in the heart of Central Texas, about 60 miles north of the state's capital city of Austin. The area boasts warm winters and hot summers. I would be there only for the summer. And, my God, was it hot!

Camp Hood was barely two years old as an Army facility. In January 1942, scarcely a month after the United States entered World War II, the War Department chose Central Texas as the wide-open spaces needed to train anti-tank forces to counter the German blitzkrieg in Europe. An initial acquisition secured 108,000 acres of cotton and cattle country. Under the rules of eminent domain, some 300 farming and ranching families were given compensation and were required, on very short notice, to give up their land. A year later, the War Department acquired an additional 50,000 acres.[4]

The mission at Camp Hood quickly expanded to include a basic training center. At times, as many as 100,000 soldiers were in training for the war effort. I was one of them. So were Jim Hise, Brenton Hirsch, "Red" Hill, Hugh Hefner, and two dozen other mostly 18-year-old recruits in Barracks # 175, whose surnames began with H.

Yes, he was *The* Hugh Hefner. In many ways, Private Hefner was just one of the boys. He did his turn at KP—peeling potatoes, scrubbing pots and pans, and serving meals—just like the rest of us. But even then he exhibited differences from those of us who grew up on farms and ranches. He was a clean-cut Chicago kid with a bent toward art. He looked really sharp in his new khakis and was very bright intellectually, but I felt that his heart was not in the Army.

Within a few days of our arrival at Camp Hood, undoubtedly

stimulated by our feeling lonely without our natural families, we began to build surrogate families. Three of us—Brenton Hirsch, Jim Hise and I—gravitated toward each other. Hirsch was a star high-school pole-vaulter from Mishawaka, Indiana. Hise was an Illinois farm boy. We remained "buddies" for the entire seventeen weeks. We talked with each other about home: our parents, siblings, girlfriends, former classmates, teammates, all the relationships that we now missed. It helped ease the pain of being away from home.

Basic Training

In his pep talk to welcome us to Camp Hood, the carbuncled, regular-army First Sergeant said, "We want you all to feel at home here. You can do here whatever you do at home. If you spit on the floor at home, spit on the floor here. *LIKE HELL*! I'm the cock of the walk around here. While you're here, you'll do as I say. Is that clear?"

In unison, several of us belted out, "Yes, Sir."

"Don't call me sir! You only say 'sir' to commissioned officers. Is that clear?"

"Old Sarg" had us all shaking in our brand-new combat boots, which I'm sure was his intent.

We recruits in Barracks # 175 spent our first ten weeks learning the very basics of soldiering. We learned to fire and care for our M-1 rifles; make our beds so they would pass the sergeant's inspection; peel potatoes, mop the floor, and scrub pots and pans while doing KP; and stay in formation and execute the sergeant's commands during drill. Then, during the next seven weeks we were to train to be Army clerks. Our group received this special status because we all had one way or another acquired proficiency in using a manual typewriter. In my case, I had taken a year of typing in high school because several pretty girls were in the class.

I felt blessed. As an Army clerk, I would be exempt from combat.

Even so, we had to learn how to disassemble, clean, and reassemble our rifles in a matter of minutes, and to fire them with precision. In this, I had a leg up on most of the mates. One of my cherished Christmas gifts had been a BB gun when I was eight years old. With it, I scared a good many sparrows and starlings. Then, when I was twelve, I inherited a hand-me-down .22 caliber rifle that I took on rabbit-hunting trips in the woods on our farm. Occasionally, I would bag a cottontail and bring it to the house for my mother to dress for supper.

My record shows that I achieved expert marksmanship status with the M-1 rifle; I have a medal to prove it. The record also indicates that I achieved expert status with the .45 caliber pistol. What the record does not show is that I was on KP the day other members of our group fired the pistols. The first and only time I ever fired a .45 was months later in the Philippines. I dreamed of a chicken dinner as I aimed and fired at a stray rooster. I missed.

Those first ten weeks at Camp Hood consisted of vigorous physical training and drill, drill, drill. For those of us who had recently experienced athletic training in high school, and who had grown up on farms wrestling 80-pound bales of hay, shoveling corn into cribs, cleaning the stables and working long hours, the physical training was a breeze. For some of the others, it was not so easy.

Once in a circle of maybe 30 guys we were asked to take turns getting on the backs of each other as we dog-trotted around the circle. One member of the group, 30-something Lester Guise, was terribly overweight, close to 300 pounds when he arrived at Camp Hood. On Army food and the heavy routine, he was changing the fat to muscle, but no one was inclined to take turns doing piggyback with Guise, so I volunteered. Guise was grateful.

Among the fitness exercises was one in which we had to dash through a series of hurdles, then run up a ramp and jump off, landing in the sand about 10 feet below. Hirsch and I enjoyed this so much we always circled around and did it a second time.

The physical training was fun. The psychological training— Killers Kollege—was not. We were taught to hate the Japs; we had to storm makeshift buildings and fire at dummy Japs with live ammunition. I detested it, but played the game. This man's army offered no choice.

Early in the time at Camp Hood, we started marching with full field pack, half a mile the first day and a bit further each day until at the end of ten weeks we did a final 20-mile march. Because of the exhausting heat, we did the final march at night. The routine was to march for 50 minutes and then take a 10-minute break, during which time the platoon leader would say, "Smoke if you've got 'em." I always gave the cigarettes from my C rations to Smitty, who was a chain smoker.

Some of the men couldn't stand the pace in that final march.

One rather frail looking guy in my squad, at about 15 miles, said apologetically that he just couldn't keep going. We encouraged him and said, "Let us carry your gear—you can make it." I carried his M-1 rifle on my left shoulder along with mine on my right. Others in the squad divided the rest of his gear among them—his cartridge belt with canteen and bayonet and his backpack. Without the gear, the guy finished the full 20 miles.

Perhaps 5 percent of the troops, including Hefner, didn't have the stamina to finish the march. They took the "meat wagon," the ambulance, the last few miles.

Weekend Pass to Austin

At the end of the first ten weeks of basic infantry training and prior to the seven weeks of specialized training, we were allowed a weekend pass. Three of us, Hirsh, Hise and I, dubbed by our barracks mates as "the three virgins," elected to take a two-hour bus ride to the state's capital city, Austin. For GIs in uniform, the ride was free.

The Three Virgins: Hesser, Hise, Hirsch

On Saturday afternoon, we roamed the streets of Austin and pigged out on junk food—hot dogs, potato chips and root beer. At the USO that night, until closing time, we danced to Big Band music with local girls whose mission was to provide morale and recreation-type services to men and women in uniform. The girls were giggly, friendly and tolerant as we awkward GIs tried to dance the jitterbug. The sponsors kept us rotating so we would not get too friendly with any one girl.

As buck privates, none of us had enough money to stay in a downtown hotel. We improvised. At a nickel a throw, we each bought a copy of the Austin newspaper, *The American Statesman*, which we spread on the ground in one of the city's parks to serve as our beds, and slept soundly.

When we awakened the next morning, we brushed ourselves off and started walking toward the center of the city. As we approached a Presbyterian church on Nueces Street, the sound of organ music reminded us of home. We decided to go in. The service was already underway, so as inconspicuously as possible we sat in a pew near the rear of the sanctuary. We three were the only ones in uniform.

After his benediction, Reverend Stanley invited the parishioners to coffee and donuts in the church's parlor.[5] He gave a special invitation to the three young soldiers. The coffee and donuts were a welcomed treat, but as an added bonus we were introduced to the pastor's attractive 17-year-old daughter, Mary Lou. As we prepared to leave, Mrs. Stanley graciously invited the three of us to the parsonage for a noontime dinner. We relished our first home-cooked meal—country-fried chicken, steaming baked potatoes and a yummy gravy—since being sworn into Uncle Sam's Army.

During the dinner conversation, Mary Lou noted that a Jimmy Cagney movie, *Yankee Doodle Dandy*, was playing at a downtown theater. With the diplomatic aplomb of an altar boy, Hirsch asked Reverend Stanley whether the three of us might take Mary Lou to see the movie. The reverend agreed.

Poor Hise was disappointed when Hirsch and I maneuvered to have Mary Lou sit between the two of us. During the entire movie, Hirsch held her left hand and I held her right. Don't tell Mary Lou, but all through the movie I imagined that I was holding Florence's hand.

In his usual self-confidence, Cagney was a captivating role-model as he portrayed the lead as a pilot in the Army Air Corps.

By the time the movie ended, it was high time for us to board the bus back to Camp Hood. As we bade good-bye to Mary Lou, at my request she put her name and address in my little black book.

Years later, when my wife Florence was flipping through the little black book, she said, "Who's this Mary Lou Stanley?" When I told her the story, Florence decided it was prudent to tear out that sheet.

As she crunched it up and threw it in the wastebasket, from memory without hesitation, I said, "1600 Nueces Street, Austin 21 Texas. Now, tear that out!"

Specialized Training

We recruits in Barracks # 175 had been told that at the end of the first ten weeks of basic training, because we could type and had scored well on the Army's entrance exam, we were to be assigned to clerks' school for the next seven weeks. However, upon finishing basic infantry training, we were informed that the Army had decided it didn't need any more clerks. We were all assigned to Anti-Tank Training, for which Camp Hood was well equipped. I did not like the change, but "This is the Army, Mr. Jones."

In teams of eight, we learned to fire 37 mm and 57 mm anti-tank guns. Team members rotated daily so that each of us would be familiar with the various tasks required to execute the firing.

37mm Gun and Crew

Following a few days' indoctrination of the mechanics of a gun, we would pull the cumbersome damned thing with a Jeep to the "battlefield" and position it in a camouflaged site, usually under the shade of tree, and play war games. A regular-Army Sergeant called the shots. The usual presumed enemy was a simulated German tank. I wondered: *Does that mean I may be going to Europe?*

All went relatively smoothly. There was not much to write home about. I looked forward to what I thought was a well-deserved 10-day furlough and wondered what my subsequent assignment would be.

During the last few days at Camp Hood, several of us in Barracks # 175 asked for autographs from those with whom we had become closest. Autograph books were common in those days. In my book, Hirsch wrote, "Met in that G.I. Chevy on June 23, 1944. No trainee ever had a better buddy. May you have the best of everything. God bless you as a soldier, and to Flossie and you the happiest life in the world."

Hise wrote, "May you and Florence have the best of everything."

Carl "Red" Hill, whom I would meet again in the Philippines, wrote, "I hope that sometime in the future we may meet to talk over the times we used to have. ...."

Guise, with whom I had taken turns carrying each other on our backs, wrote, "Remember the Camp Hood Campaign!"

Hefner's entry was different. He showed artistic ability as he took time to draw a caricature of a perspiring GI Joe with full pack. He signed it "Hef." I still have it.

Hugh Hefner's cartoon

Ten-Day Furlough

At the end of the seventeen weeks of basic training, I packed my duffle bag, donned dress khakis, and boarded a train to Winchester, Indiana.

My parents, grandparents, sister, aunts and uncles all treated me like a hero—as if I had already won the war. Florence and I were together constantly. She went with me to meet and spend time with various relatives, including my dear grandparents John and Ida Bolinger. I also became better acquainted with her parents, Chester and Nellie Life, her brother Hugh Jacob, and her sister-in-law Virginia.

In an effort to get better acquainted with her farmer-turned-soldier friend, Florence's father invited me to the offices of the Life Manufacturing Company for a chat. Although I had met him briefly before, I was nervous. With all the courage I could muster I told Mr. Life that I was very much in love with his daughter and pleaded for his consent to marry her after the war.

Following the session, Mr. Life gave a crisp assessment to Mrs. Life: "Well, one thing's for sure, Leon is no bullshitter!"

Mother Life was softening. She recognized that she would have to accept the inevitable. Mr. Life gave his consent.

Newly engaged Leon and Florence with Mother, sister Vivian, Father and cousin Wanda

Even though I had only recently turned 19, my parents, who deeply admired Florence, seemed pleased when I told them that I had gone to Webb's Jewelry store in Winchester and bought an engagement ring.

When the two of us were alone that night, listening to dreamy music in the parlor of the Life family's beautiful Colonial home, I slipped the ring on Florence's finger as I kissed her. She cried. We knew that, at best, it would be many months before the war would be over, but we were deeply in love—we would anticipate the moment when we could be together again.

To pay for the ring, I had invested two month's salary as a buck private. Florence's sister-in-law, Virginia, squinted to see the diamond as she said, "Isn't it cute!"

Florence was as happy with the ring as if the diamond were two carats.

On the last night of my home leave, Florence and I spent some precious time alone, in my father's car, parked in a secluded, wooded area beside Fudge's gravel pit, just outside Winchester's city limits. A nearly-full moon illuminated the contours of Florence's fine-featured face. We cuddled for more than an hour, neither of us saying a word. For the first time, I touched her breasts. We both cried. Those treasured moments remained crystal-clear in my mind while I was overseas.

Early the next morning, my parents drove me in Dad's 1939 Ford to Richmond, Indiana, where I took a four-day, non-sleeper train ride to the replacement depot at Camp Stoneman, California, to await orders. Most of us who were 19 or older when we finished basic training had orders to go to Camp Stoneman after the leave. Hirsch, Hise and Hefner, who were still 18, were not yet subject to going overseas.

I had a toothache for the entire four-day train ride. The Army dentist was less-than-patient as he pulled the tooth soon after I arrived at Stoneman on Sunday, his normal day of rest.

Worse than the toothache, though, was leaving Florence behind.

Chapter 3: 34-day Ocean Voyage to the Philippines

In mid-December 1944, I was one of 3,145 Army-troop replacements who sailed under San Francisco's Golden Gate Bridge aboard the USS *General R. L. Howze* for destinations unknown, at least so far as we buck privates were concerned. The replacements consisted of 227 officers and 2,918 male enlisted men. Among the officers were 21 nurses and 60 WAACs (Women's Army Auxiliary Corps).[6]

I had never before seen an ocean.

The fourth day at sea, we passed near enough to the Hawaiian Islands that we could see their profiles on the horizon. At about that point, the ship's cook served us a dinner of greasy pork. The sea became a bit choppy. Many of the passengers, and even some of the sailors, spent long hours heaving over the edge of the deck. For a time, I was woozy and had to lie down, but I never fed the fishes.

Early in the voyage, in response to the enticement that volunteers would receive three meals each day rather than two, I volunteered for kitchen duty. My job each day was to work with a crew that moved dozens of cartons of supplies from the hold below onto an elevator and up to the galley. One day, as inconspicuously as possible, I set aside one of the cartons. Later, I picked it up and took it to the sleeping quarters. When my buddies and I opened the carton, we found that it contained four one-gallon tin cans of peaches. For each of the next four days, we savored a gallon of canned peach halves as an after-dinner treat.

The *General Howze* was one of more than 2,000 Liberty ships, known as the workhorses of World War II. They were simple, square-hulled vessels welded and hammered together by the hundreds. President Roosevelt called them "dreadful looking objects." The press called them "American ugly ducklings." Construction from keel to completion took an average of less than two months for each ship.

The *Howze*, built by Kaiser Shipbuilding Inc. in Richmond, California, was launched on May 23, 1943. She was christened in honor of Major General Robert L. Howze, a veteran of the Spanish-American war who received the Distinguished Service Medal for World War I service. She had an 8,500 horsepower engine, displaced 17,250 tons, and had a top speed of 22 knots. She had 356 officers and crew and a troop capacity of 3,530.

Until she was decommissioned after the war, the *General Howze* carried troops, supplies, and even Japanese prisoners of war on eleven voyages to and from combat areas in the Pacific. On this particular voyage, the ship followed a zig-zag path, changing course ever-so-slightly after 10-minute intervals, to avoid detection by enemy submarines. It took about 12 minutes for a well-trained submarine crew to develop a "fire control solution," to get a fix on a surface craft, so if the ship changed course during that interval, the enemy submarine crew would have to recalculate before they fired a torpedo.

To pass time, I would read, or play cards, or do calisthenics. I often stood near the railing on the main deck and gazed toward the distant horizon. I was fascinated for hours at a time by the flying fish, the dolphins, the multicolored giant eels, and other strange creatures of the sea.

I was overwhelmed as I thought about what the future might bring. I would think, *Okay, so I'm someplace in the Pacific. Where in hell are we headed? Could I be going into battle, with only four months of training? I'm scared. I'm really scared.*

Life on Board

Space on the ship was limited. Rather than sit to eat our meals, we stood elbow-to-elbow beside long, narrow "tables" about 12 or 14 inches wide. In rough seas, we had to hold our trays to keep them from sliding, and we would lean against the table to maintain our balance.

The ship's holds had rows and rows of canvas bunks, five deep, with about a 24-inch space between each one. My bunk was on the bottom. The hold was getting warmer and warmer as we headed south. We crossed the Equator on Christmas Eve. It was so hot by that time that perspiration dripped on me from the men in the bunks above.

It was a tradition in the Navy that a raucous and rowdy "Davy Jones" initiation was in store for those sailors who were crossing the Equatorial line for the first time. Sailors who had crossed the line before were known as shellbacks, or Sons of Neptune. The eldest shellback was called King Neptune, the mythological god of the sea, and the next eldest was his assistant, Davy Jones.

We Army replacements were privileged to watch the "pollywogs" be smeared, dunked, and otherwise harassed by King Neptune and the shellbacks who had previously crossed the Equator. The pollywogs had to kneel and say a prayer while the shellbacks paddled them. Next, they were smeared from head to toe with grease and paint, followed by a skinhead haircut. Then, they were placed over a big gun and asked to sing while being paddled, following which they were tossed headfirst into a tank of water and dunked until they could yell, "Shellback," when they emerged. Watching them made me feel glad to be in the Army rather than the Navy.

Rumors of our destination were rampant throughout the 34-day voyage. Among the more prominent—and the one that many of us wanted to believe—was the "straight poop" that we were headed for Borneo to be assigned to a "Labor Battalion;" we simply had not had enough training to be sent directly into combat.

Little did we know.

At about three weeks into our voyage, the Captain of the *Howze* dropped anchor for a few days at Oro Bay, Papua/New Guinea, to await orders. During those two or three days, a few of us at a time were taken by small boats to the beach for a swim. We had no swimming suits, so we skinny dipped. While three buddies and I, stark naked, were wading out to sea in water about two feet deep, a Jeep-load of WAACs passed along the beach. We all four faced the young ladies, and waved. Years later, when one of my wife's friends was telling me she had been a WAAC and was stationed for a time on New Guinea, I told her of my little escapade on the beach. With animated gestures, she said, "Oh, I remember that. Now, I recognize you!"

Several hours after the *Howze* departed New Guinea we troops were informed by officers on board that we were headed for Leyte, where General Douglas MacArthur and his forces had landed on October 20, 1944. Together with 839 other replacements aboard ship—796 enlisted men and 43 officers—I was told that I would be assigned to the 34th Infantry Regiment of the 24th Division. The 24th was known as the Victory Division. It had fought many battles and lost none.

Our mission: to avenge the atrocities of Bataan.

Background on Bataan

I had had a glimpse of MacArthur's triumphant return to the Philippines in a newsreel at the Lyric Theater in Winchester while I was on home leave. He was a flamboyant, colorful figure as he waded ashore on the island of Leyte.

The Philippines had become an important dimension of Douglas MacArthur's life. His first assignment, after graduating at the top of

37

his class from West Point in 1903, was in the Philippines, where his father had served as military governor just two years before. Douglas had a second tour there in 1923-24. In the late 1920s, he went again to the Philippines where he served as department commander until, at age 50, he returned to the U.S. in 1930 as chief of staff of the Army and was promoted to full General.

In 1936, General MacArthur was appointed military advisor to the Philippines, where he trained military forces and prepared the Philippine government for its coming independence. In 1937, he retired from the Army, but remained in the Philippines as an advisor to its government.

In the summer of 1941, the entire Philippine Army was inducted into the Army of the United States and, at age 61, MacArthur was recalled to active duty to head the new command: U.S. Forces in the Far East.

At 0530 Manila time on December 8, 1941, General George C. Marshall, who was chief-of-staff of the Army and a longtime rival of MacArthur, called him by scrambler telephone in Manila and said, "Pearl Harbor has been bombed. We are at war with Japan. They are closer to you than they are to Hawaii. You had better be on the alert. Get your planes up in the air. Get everybody on alert and be on a war footing."

At about 0900, hundreds of Japanese army bombers from Formosa were spotted over Northern Luzon, headed toward Manila.

For whatever reason, MacArthur failed to alert his air force. As a result, the destruction of U.S. aircraft on the ground, mostly B-17 Flying Fortresses and P-40s, was catastrophic.

After General MacArthur left the Philippines on March 11, 1942 to establish his command post in Australia, President Roosevelt named General Jonathan Wainwright as commander of all U.S. forces in the Philippine theater. The following day, Wainwright placed General Ed King in charge of all Filipino and American forces on Luzon.

When the Japanese learned that MacArthur had fled, they dropped leaflets promising good treatment for those who surrendered. With his forces on Luzon terribly outnumbered, with inadequate food, medical supplies and equipment, General King recognized the inevitable. On April 2, the Japanese began a final offensive with massive air and artillery bombardments. After four days of intense fighting, General King believed that no sane man could consider anything but surrender. Defying Wainwright's direct order to "counter attack," and in the belief that it would prevent a bloodbath, on April 8 King surrendered his troops on Bataan: 66,000 Filipinos and 12,000 Americans. This was the largest contingent of U.S. Army troops ever to surrender to a foreign entity. Rather than the promised "good treatment" came the Bataan Death March.

Lt. General Masaharu Homma, the Japanese officer in charge, was perplexed about how to handle this many prisoners. He had instructions from Tokyo on how to deal with 25,000 prisoners, not the more than 78,000 that he now had on his hands. That worried him. How would he feed them? He didn't have enough food, water, medicine, or transport for his own men. How could he possibly care for this many prisoners?

Homma's solution: By the time they arrived at the prisoner of war camps on the Bataan Peninsula, sixty-five to eighty-five miles north, there had to be a lot fewer POWs. He marched the captives to the prison camps with virtually no food or water. If they complained, they were tortured; many were killed with bayonets. The march became a brutal, unorganized extermination. For those who survived the march, the anguish continued in the prison camps. Most of the prisoners, American and Filipino alike, were tortured, starved, shot, or worked until they expired.

The Bataan Death March and its aftermath turned out to be one of the darkest episodes of World War II.

The Japanese had accepted the unconditional surrender of General King's troops on Bataan. General Wainwright was still holding out on the small fortress island of Corregidor. Wainwright vowed to fight on. The Japanese pounded it with air strikes, naval gunfire, and artillery. By May 6, Corregidor's holdouts could endure no more. General Wainwright surrendered unconditionally.

(Because General Homma's completing the capture of the Philippines took longer than the 50 days allowed by Imperial Japanese Headquarters and after the last American forces had surrendered, on Corregidor, Homma was recalled to Japan in August 1942. In January 1946 he was tried by the U.S. Military Commission for the many war crimes committed by his men, including the Bataan Death March. He was executed by a firing squad on April 3, 1946.)

Chapter 4: MacArthur Returns

After the Japanese attack on Pearl Harbor on December 7, 1941, Chester W. Nimitz was appointed commander in chief of the Pacific Fleet, a command that brought both land and sea forces under his authority. By June 1942, Admiral Nimitz had overseen the decisive victory at the Battle of Midway. Subsequently, he directed the historic battles of the Solomon Islands, the Marshall Islands, and the Marianas, which could then serve as stepping stones for larger objectives.

While I was still in training at Camp Hood, we learned that U.S. troops had successfully re-conquered the chain of Mariana Islands in the Pacific. The airfields there, once they were rehabilitated, served our planes that could now reach Japan with relative ease. We replacements were not aware of it at the time, but while we were on the *Howze* the first B-29s were taking off from the Marianas to bomb the Japanese mainland for the first time since Jimmy Doolittle's raid in 1942. It was a morale booster when we learned about it.

By 1944, when I entered the service, the United States had more than ten million men in uniform. American industry, which included millions of women who had not previously worked in industry, was turning out planes, tanks, ships and weapons sufficient to fight in the Pacific as well as in Europe.

American carrier aircraft had bombed Japan's air force practically out of existence. U.S. Navy submarines, operating from bases in New Guinea, New Britain, and the Marianas, were sinking Japanese merchant ships and crude oil carriers faster than they could be replaced.

While I was still at Camp Hood, though we were unaware at the time, President Franklin D. Roosevelt met secretly in Hawaii in July 1944 with General MacArthur and Admiral Nimitz to develop a strategy to defeat Japan. It was not a comfortable meeting. Operational control of the Pacific theater was divided between MacArthur as commander of the South West Pacific area and Nimitz as commander of the Pacific Ocean areas. Inter-service rivalry between the Army and Navy was amplified by the personal enmity between the two commanders.

One of the issues was whether the strategy should be to retake the Philippines, or to isolate them and go directly to islands closer to Japan, such as Formosa or Okinawa. MacArthur made a strong case that the next step should be the Philippines.

After the briefing, as commander in chief, the President decided that the Philippines would be the next major offensive. Then, if the Japanese did not surrender unconditionally, Japan's Home Islands would be invaded.

When the time came to invade the Philippines, General MacArthur decided that the first assault would be on the island of Leyte, toward the middle of the Philippine archipelago. On October 15, 1944, Allied amphibious forces rendezvoused at the north end of the Surigao Strait, just east of Leyte. The 738-ship armada was the most powerful naval force ever assembled for battle. In addition to the troop ships, it included eight large aircraft carriers, twenty-four small carriers, a dozen battleships, two dozen cruisers, and 141 destroyers.

The ships' heavy guns and more than 1,000 carrier aircraft swept the beaches in preparation for landing. For three days prior to the landing, our Navy minesweepers cleared the area of underwater mines. Morton Eisenberg, currently my neighbor in Naples, Florida, was a Navy seaman on the bridge of the minesweeper USS *Howard* at the time. Surreptitiously, he kept a diary. It reads, in part:

October 17: Had unidentified aircraft overhead. Weather is terribly rough and typhoon is blowing. Heavy rain and every place flooded. At 0200 rendezvoused with cruisers and destroyers and commenced sweeping at 0600. We were to sweep Leyte Gulf … At 0820 Rangers landed on Suluan Is. Killed 32 Japs and lost 2 men. … 100 friendly natives greeted Rangers on Suluan. (Sister minesweeper) USS *Crosby* lost man overboard. … Put in 6 ½ hours on wheel. Retired for night.

October 18: at 0500 commenced sweeping … Weather has improved greatly. Had 4 hours sleep last night on wet deck in soaked clothes. Passed four Filipinos close abroad in canoe with sail. They saluted and greeted us.

October 19: Followed other sweepers as demolition ship. Mine exploded near us on our beam. Many mines were being cut loose. *Palmer* lost man overboard but he was recovered. … Ship reported canoe with women and children. USS *Ross* beached after hitting 2 mines. 20 men were killed. 2 Jap planes bombed *Ross* injuring 2 men. No direct hits on ship. Jap fighter came close off our bow … Planes chased him away. Destroyed and sunk 7 more mines in afternoon. Enemy dive bombers dropped bombs on our formation near the USS *Hovey* … Destroyed our 10th mine in evening. Retired in evening.[7]

Early on the morning of October 20, MacArthur and Vice Admiral Thomas Kinkaid, who was in charge of naval forces under MacArthur's command, agreed that the beaches had been sufficiently prepared to land the troops. MacArthur was told that the headquarters of the Japanese 16th Division had likely been destroyed. He is said to have remarked, "Good, that's the outfit that did the dirty work on Bataan."

Shortly before dawn, Kinkaid gave the order: "Land the landing force."

The 96th and 24th Infantry Divisions led the assault. Well before noon, soldiers of the 96th had captured Hill 120 and the 24th moved inland. The 16,000 Japanese troops on Leyte, a fraction of the total of 270,000 in the Philippines, were short on supplies, ammunition and fuel. But they fought with determination.

Shortly after noon, a Navy landing craft motored to within a few feet of the beach. It let down its ramp, and with bullets snapping through the air a few hundred meters away, General Douglas MacArthur strode through the shallow water to the shore. The old general had kept his promise.

MacArthur headed to the 24th Infantry Division's command post where he broadcast a message to the Filipino people and to listeners in America: "This is the voice of freedom. People of the Philippines, I have returned."

First Lieutenant Paul Austin served in the assault with the 2nd Battalion, 34th Infantry Regiment, 24th Division. He landed on Leyte at about the same time and place as did General MacArthur. In Oliver North's *War Stories II*, Lt. Austin reports:

> Then I heard a loud voice to my left. He said, "Let's get off this beach! Follow me!"
>
> General MacArthur came in [in] the same area we did. … When MacArthur waded ashore right behind our battalion, the word went just like wildfire. "MacArthur has landed!" kept going through the ranks. Everybody knew who he was, and it was uplifting.
>
> We had heard that phrase "I shall return" over and over. It was kind of a motto, something for us to look forward to.[8]

Lt. Austin continued: "About one o'clock that morning [October 21] ... all hell broke loose. As it turned out, two of our platoons were caught in a banzai attack, and they hit G Company something awful. ...

"I had about 180 guys in my rifle company when we landed on Leyte. When we left, there were fifty-five men left."[9]

G Company was to be my new outfit.[a]

Retaking Leyte

The Battle of Leyte Gulf—the largest naval battle in history—was a four-day affair in which the Japanese lost almost half of their naval forces to the American Navy. From October 24 to 27, more than 10,500 Japanese sailors and airmen were killed. Even more profound, from a strategic standpoint, was the loss of 28 of their 64 ships, including four aircraft carriers, three battleships, ten cruisers and eleven destroyers. The Americans lost six ships.[10]

Meanwhile, it was tough going for the American soldiers on the island of Leyte. In early November, the Japanese brought in 13,000 reinforcements. On a hill called "Breakneck Ridge," ten days of combat from November 7 to 17 were among the bloodiest of the entire war. Soldiers of the 24th Division used everything they had—rifles, machine guns, flame-throwers and hand grenades—and finally prevailed; some 2,000 Japanese soldiers died on that infamous hill. So did many Americans.

By early December nearly all of the enemy soldiers on Leyte had been killed or captured and the island was finally secured by U.S. troops. The 75 days of grueling combat on Leyte cost the Japanese more than 70,000 lives; some 15,500 Americans were killed or wounded as General Douglas MacArthur kept his promise to return to the Philippines.

Victory Division

The 24th Infantry, known as the "Victory Division," is one of the few divisions that specialize in assault spearheads in tropical terrain. The Division's three regiments were the 19th, the 21st, and the 34th. I was to be assigned to the 34th.

---

a   See Appendices A and B for information on soldiers' ranks and the structure of Army units.

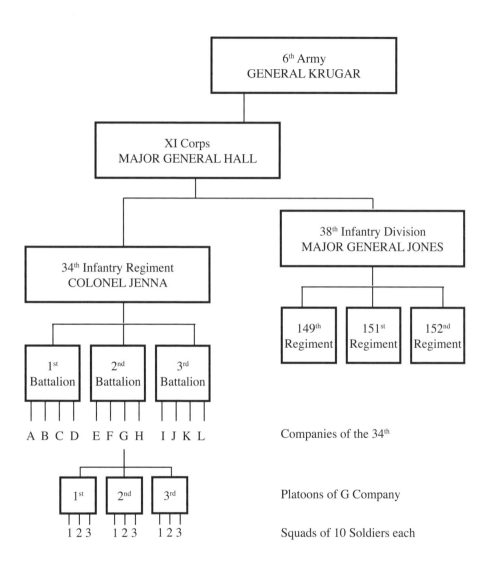

Military organisation chart...

The 34th Infantry Regiment had three battalions. First Battalion was composed of companies A, B, C and D; Second Battalion included companies E, F, G and H; and Third Battalion had companies I, J, K and L. I was destined to be a rifleman in G Company, 2ⁿᵈ Battalion.

G Company, under command of Captain Ben Wahle, had been involved in two major battles on Leyte. Wahle's company was in the second wave to invade. Their first night on Leyte was a nightmare. The Japanese lost 600 men in the encounter early the next morning. G Company, which took the hardest blows, had 14 killed and 12 wounded. Subsequently, Wahle and his troops were cut off for 17 days south of Capoocan during the battle of Breakneck Ridge. The 24ᵗʰ Division History states: "The saga of company 'G' in maintaining a ridge-top blocking position over more than three weeks played a key role in the success on Breakneck Ridge. … Supplies began to grow short, making a diet of coconuts and rainwater necessary. The stench of decaying bodies fouled the air."[11]

My Place in Victory Division
The rugged survivors of the 75-day battle looked at us tender-footed, pink-skinned replacements with a great deal of skepticism when we off-loaded from the *General Howze*. The Filipinos were more gracious; they gave us the "V" sign. Children called out, "Victory Joe!"

The majority of Filipinos are descendants of migrants from Taiwan during the Iron Age. Vibrant and charming, they are relatively small in stature. Young Filipinos could shinny up a coconut palm with the dexterity of an Olympic tumbler. They crowded around us GIs and asked questions to learn more about their liberators and, while doing so, to practice their English. One young man, who looked to be at least as old as I, looked up at me curiously and asked how old I was. When I said, "I'm 19," he shook his head in disbelief and said, "No, you have to be older than that; how old are you, really?"

As a veritable morale builder, we had the first mail call since leaving California. I had several letters from Florence and a few from my sister and my parents. In return, I wrote letters to them. We used Victory Mail, called "V-Mail," during those wartime years. Although quite limited in space for messages, they were much faster in transit than regular mail. After brief letters had been written on compact V-Mail forms, they were photographed and put on film, flown across the world and then reproduced at the mail center closest to the recipient's position. Transit time was 12 days or less, compared with six weeks by ship, and weight was reduced by 98 percent compared with paper letters.

For security reasons, our mail was censored by commissioned officers. Against all rules, my letter to Florence from Leyte contained a coded message. It was not a sophisticated code. Since Leyte was much in the news back home, my coded letter must have conveyed a discomforting message for Florence and my parents. Now that more than 60 years have passed, I feel safe in divulging the code: When I ended a letter by saying simply, 'Love, Leon,' Florence was to take the first letter of each paragraph to spell the name of the location where I was at the time.

January 22, 1945
Dearest Florence:

Let me call you sweetheart, I'm in love with you ...

Every time I think of you, I sing that song to myself.

Yes, I still love you, and I always will.

Tonight, my two buddies and I are going to a movie. I think it's a cowboy show; Hopalong Cassidy is the star.

Each time I go to a movie, I think of the times when we went to the Lyric and held hands. Gotta go now.

Love,

At dusk on the second evening on Leyte, we saw a "Betty" bomber go chugging by. The two-engine Betty, the main "heavy" bomber of the Japanese Navy, was remarkable at the time for its long range, which was achieved by its having huge fuel tanks in the wings but no heavy armor. In addition to the nickname Betty, Americans called it the "Flying Cigar," a parody on its shape, or "One-Shot Lighter," because it tended to explode with as little as one well-aimed barrage.

Hot on that Betty's trail was one of the Army Air Corps' new

P-61 Black Widow fighter planes, the first U.S. aircraft designed to be a night fighter. Equipped with radar, it was an extremely capable and deadly craft.

A flash in the distant horizon signaled the end of that Flying Cigar.

We were on Leyte for just a few days before leaving for the next assignment: Luzon. The old-timers suggested that we throw away our gas masks; the Japanese had given no indication that they had the capability to use gas as a weapon. We gladly tossed them. But before tossing mine, at the suggestion of a battle-worn sergeant, I cut off a rubber link from the hose of my mask and fitted it around my dog tag. It would keep the tag from clinking and giving away our position when we were close to the enemy.

From Leyte to Luzon

The Leyte campaign had been the biggest campaign in the Pacific to date. That record was about to be shattered, with the invasion of Luzon, the northernmost and largest of the Philippine Islands. MacArthur's largest and costliest operations were to occur on Luzon. About 250,000 Japanese soldiers were prepared for a major, perhaps final, confrontation. They would fight to their death.

On January 24th, 1945, the day I boarded ship in Tacloban Harbor, Leyte, to embark for Luzon, the 34th Infantry Regiment received replacements of 43 officers and 796 enlisted men, including myself, who had arrived in the Philippines a few days earlier aboard the *General Howze*. The additions brought the regiment, under command of Colonel William Jenna, to 3,001 soldiers, nearly to the full strength that it had been before the Leyte campaign. Despite our youth and limited training, we would have to do. The regiment sorely needed the replacements.

Author David Mann suggests that "The sudden influx of new second lieutenants in the 34th must have deflated more than one veteran platoon sergeant. These sergeants had led their platoons through thick and thin for months; now they had to hand over their platoons to young, '120-day wonders.'"[1] The Army allotted 120 days to train an officer inductee to become an officer. Many thought it took a great deal longer to truly become an officer.

Together with several other pink-skinned recruits, I was assigned as a rifleman to one of the three platoons of G Company, 2nd Battalion, 34th Infantry Regiment. Carl "Red" Hill, who had been a barracks mate at Camp Hood, went to F Company. Second Lieutenant Paul G. Silber, one of the "120-day wonders" who came over on the *Howze*, was assigned as a G Company platoon leader.

It took approximately 60 hours for the convoy of aircraft carriers, battleships, cruisers, destroyers, oilers, cargo ships, personnel carriers, minesweepers, and landing craft, to go the 800-mile route from Leyte to the west coast of Luzon. We replacements, who had not yet had a chance to test-fire our newly issued rifles, nervously passed the time by thoroughly cleaning our weapons, which we had inherited from compatriots who were killed or wounded on Leyte. The chilling thought that I might meet the same fate was imbedded in my mind. The invincibility that I enjoyed before and during basic training was fading fast.

As the American convoy entered the waters off Luzon under a full moon on January 28, the night before the scheduled assault, Colonel Jenna broadcast this message to all his troops over the ships' loud speakers:

> The 34th ... has a most important mission. The commanding general of this task force has placed his entire faith in this regiment of veterans, which proved its worth at Hollandia, Biak and Leyte. We will not let him down. Hit hard and destroy the Japs. Drive fast and go through to our objective. May God's blessing be on us and may His strength and courage carry us to a quick and complete victory.[13]

Colonel Jenna could not have conceived of the defensive stronghold that the Japanese had built in the wild terrain of ZigZag Pass.

Map of Philippines

Chapter 5: Three Days in ZigZag Pass

General MacArthur's grand plan was to open up Manila Bay by securing the Bataan Peninsula and the islands, principally Corregidor, guarding the entrance to the Bay. Clearing ZigZag Pass was crucial to that effort.

> ZigZag Pass was not lightly named. There is no map to show but half the twists and circles, the dips and rises, the strong slopes, the cliffs and gorges that make it hazardous and difficult fighting ground. Each turn masked the road beyond. Having passed one turn, the road was visible only to the next.
> The Jap was getting rough. ...[14]

ZigZag Pass is about 30 miles north of the southern tip of the Bataan peninsula. From the port of Olongapo on Subic Bay on the west coast of Luzon, the pass runs 14 miles east along Philippine National Highway 7 to the strategic city of Dinalupihan. The pass follows a zig-zag pattern through elevated, densely overgrown terrain in the inhospitable mountains surrounding the central Luzon plain. Highway 7 is the only road connecting Subic Bay and Manila.

The job of taking control of the pass was assigned to XI Corps, made up of four infantry regiments. Besides the 34th Infantry Regiment, the corps included the untried 38th Division, which had two National Guard infantry regiments from Indiana and one from Kentucky. The 34th was experienced in battle, but because of its heavy casualties in the 75-day Leyte campaign, 40 percent of the infantry troops, including myself, were new replacements. Major General Charles Hall, whom the old-timers described as tough, hard-nosed and uncompromising, was XI Corps commander.

Two hours before dawn on January 29, our convoy of ships anchored about four miles off the west coast of Luzon. Wardrooms of the transports were converted into surgeries. Doctors stood by.

Early that morning, the Navy served us bacon and eggs. At 0500, we lined up to board landing crafts. I wore my helmet and carried at least 50 pounds of weapons and gear, including mess kit, a poncho, and a change of underwear and socks. Fastened to my cartridge belt, in addition to eight-round clips of ammunition, were a water canteen, first aid packet, entrenching tool, and bayonet.

The .30-caliber Garand, semi-automatic M-1 rifle, which weighs 9 ½ pounds, gave us a decided advantage over the Japanese, who were still firing a bolt action, five-clip rifle of World War I vintage.

One man in each squad of ten soldiers carried a .30 caliber Browning Automatic Rifle (BAR), a cross between a rifle and a machine gun. With bipod and magazine, the gas-operated BAR weighs 19 pounds. The BAR man normally carried twelve 20-round magazines in a special cartridge belt with six pouches of two magazines each. The BAR, which could fire 300 to 350 rounds per minute, was particularly potent for close fighting in the jungle. As I would learn shortly, the BAR man was a prime target for enemy snipers.

On the morning of the landing, air cover was provided by Army Air Corps planes from Leyte: P-47 Thunderbolts and twin-fuselage P-38s equipped with a 20-mm cannon and four 50-caliber machine guns. It had been planned that the Navy would bombard the coast for about an hour prior to the scheduled landing of troops. However, reconnaissance indicated that Filipino and American flags were flying on the beach. Artillery was withheld.

When the landing boats dropped their ramps in the sand, Filipinos met us and, with much emotion, thanked us for coming. They waved American flags. One agile Filipino climbed a tree and threw down coconuts for the liberators.

No Japanese were waiting for us on "Blue Beach." They had withdrawn to the hills of ZigZag Pass, leaving a trail of burning bridges. Our engineers quickly built emergency bridges. Bulldozers scooped out fords for the heavier traffic.

The Japanese war plan had changed following the Battle of Leyte. Rather than try with all the firepower they had to keep their enemy from coming ashore, which brought their beach defenses to a shambles, they would let the invaders come ashore and then try to overcome them from well-dug-in, fortified positions in the hills of the hinterland.

Under command of Major Harry L. Snavely, the 2nd Battalion of the 34th, to which I was assigned, was the initial spearhead of the corps' advance. Filipino guerillas reported no Japanese along the first stretch of Highway 7, so 2nd Battalion moved fast. Snavely led his men in a forced foot march through southern Zambales. The day was hot and dry. The sun-baked roads followed long-dried stream beds. By the end of the first day, we had hiked 12 miles through two towns. Many of the troops sagged from heat exhaustion.

All along the way, Filipinos greeted us with handfuls of flowers. At a bivouac in the wooded hills near Subic Town, at the top of Subic Bay, we dug in for the night.

From Subic Town, all-weather Highway 7 twists south for six miles, hugging the coast, to the port of Olongapo before turning east toward Dinalupihan. The vanguard passed the village of San Antonio and struck Highway 7, a road with a solid crown. The next day, guerrilla guides reported for duty before dawn. We ate K-ration breakfasts in starlit darkness. Colonel Jenna picked the 3rd Battalion 34th to lead the advance to Olongapo. The bridges across the Matain and Matagan Rivers were still afire. The forward troops forded the streams.

Our 2nd Battalion remained at bivouac until mid-day, then proceeded to half-way between Subic Town and Olongapo, where we dug in for the second night. We had K rations for dinner. Next morning, we had K rations again. No one complained.

We learned later that since we had landed on Luzon, a daring mission of four officers and 121 volunteers had rescued 500 American POWs from a Japanese prison camp on the island. That news helped give our own mission a shot of adrenalin.

Under pressure from his two bosses—Generals MacArthur and Krueger—General Hall deemed that speed was essential in getting through ZigZag Pass to secure Dinalupihan. General Hall thought that the pass was lightly defended; he expected his troops to be through the pass and in Dinalupihan by February 5. He must have been pleased with the first two days of operation. More than 35,000 troops had landed and thousands of tons of supplies had been unloaded. He was confident of finishing his work in northern Bataan by the target date.

Japanese troops defending the pass—slightly more than 2,000— had chosen their position well. With fanatic zeal and determination, they would defend every inch of ZigZag Pass. At the Kalaklan River bridge they had dug machinegun bunkers and trenches. A solitary Japanese crept onto the bridge from its southern end. His mission, apparently, was demolition. From 800 yards away, the muzzle of a Garand traced his movement. Steady behind the Garand's sights peered the eye of a Yankee sergeant. The Garand barked. The Jap dropped. The sergeant fired again to make sure. That opened the battle for Bataan.[15]

The tangled growth of the jungle flora along Highway 7 was so thick that one dare not step more than two or three yards off to the side; he would not be able to see the road. It was easy to imagine a Nip behind every tree or bush.

At 0845 on February 1, Japanese light machine guns—we called them "woodpeckers"—pinned down troops of the 152nd Regiment. The commander called forth two Sherman tanks. They silenced the machine guns, but the Japanese had already demonstrated well their determination to make a stand. The lead regiment suffered 43 wounded and 14 killed. At dawn on February 2, casualties were brought down the road from the Pass. It was impossible to move the wounded during the night.

Filipino guerrillas and Negritos, the pygmy people of Luzon who served as guides on our way to Dinalupihan, carried food, water and ammunition to the front lines. Some of them carried a complete portable surgical hospital on their backs. It would be put to good use.

Our 2nd Battalion 34th saw little action until February 3. During the three-day interim, several units of the 38th Division rotated back and forth at the front. Confusion reigned. Ambulances churned in relays between the field hospitals and the front. Truckloads of dead rolled back for military burial.

History suggests that "Japanese morale reached its zenith after the repulse of the 152nd" on both February 1 and 2.[16] These Japanese were not the rear echelon troops that General Hall and the XI Corps staff thought were defending ZigZag Pass. They were skilled and tenacious. They had a solid wall of strong defenses on dominating terrain.

Sensing that the advance of the 152nd was not going well, General Hall and his staff unfolded an action plan that he hoped would solve his problem. He would replace the 152nd Infantry with the veteran 34th and place the 34th directly under XI Corps control. But the 34th was not the same battle-hardened regiment that had spearheaded the attack across the northern part of Leyte; men who had lived together, trained together and fought together for months.

The regiment had suffered 748 casualties on Leyte. Among the casualties was the regimental commander, Aubrey S. Newman, who was wounded severely in the stomach. Newman's replacement, Colonel Jenna, was less experienced. The 839 replacements, most of us fresh from basic training, had no experience with each other or in unit training. We had only one week's acquaintance with the regulars of the 34th prior to combat. Squad leaders hardly had time to learn the names of us new men before we headed for ZigZag Pass.

As he retired for the night, General Hall radioed General Krueger: "I am putting my faith in Colonel Jenna and the 34th."[17]

The Japanese had set up defensive positions on ridgelines perpendicular to the road, beginning about three miles east of Olongapo and continuing east for about 4,000 yards along Highway 7. Conquering that two-mile stretch—the Battle of ZigZag Pass— turned out to be bloody for both the Japanese and the Americans. The Japanese troops

> had constructed an elaborate system of interconnecting pillboxes, caves and trenches ... and had stocked them with abundant food and ammunition. ... an extensive trench system connected major points, enabling the defenders to move from one position to another unobserved. ... an experienced observer, who had been on Saipan, stated that the defenses ... were the most extensive he had seen.[18]

The next three days were to become the most memorable and frightening of my entire life.

February 3

About 2:30 on the morning of February 3, Colonel Jenna relayed to his battalion commanders the orders sent down by XI Corps. The 34th was to: PASS THROUGH LEADING ELEMENTS 38TH INFANTRY DIVISION IN THEIR PRESENT POSITIONS AND ATTACK VIGOROUSLY DIRECTION DINALUPIHAN.

The 34th would be reinforced by a tank company and a detachment from an engineering battalion. A dozen Filipino guerillas from Corps Headquarters would help guide the operation to smash through the Japanese imbedded along Highway 7.

Colonel Jenna designated the 1st Battalion to lead the attack; 2nd and 3rd Battalions would follow in a convoy of fifty 2 ½ ton, "6x6," trucks. Along with others in G Company, I boarded a 6x6 at Olongapo at 0700 and we began the gradual ascent to the battleground. As we proceeded, the denseness and darkness of the jungle cast a foretelling gloom. Most of the troops in my 6x6 inhaled heavily as they smoked their K-ration cigarettes. Under my breath, I said a quick prayer. I thought about Florence.

At 0930, 1st Battalion 34th moved forward to enter ZigZag Pass on a half-mile loop in Highway 7 known as "the horseshoe." That great loop contained a dozen little loops, each of which changed the direction of the road ever so slightly, but enough that lead scouts could not see the solid wall of strong defenses on dominating terrain around the next turn, or the next, or the next. The banks on the left side of the road jutted steeply upward; deep gullies were on the right side.

When 1st Battalion pushed around the horseshoe, they came upon a tank trap—a huge tree felled across the road; the tree was mined on both sides. As our tanks approached the area, "kamikaze" soldiers hidden in holes beside the road, each with an explosive meant to destroy a tank, made a dash toward the tanks. Soldiers from 1st Battalion who were walking beside the tanks killed three of the attackers with rifle fire and grenades. A fourth was killed by the premature explosion of his own bomb. Engineers were called to eliminate the tank trap. Luckily, none of our tanks was harmed.

Highway 7 became a tangled mess as three battalions of the 152nd Regiment were retiring at the same time that the three battalions of the 34th were approaching the Pass. Taking advantage of the confusion, Major Ogawa, commander of Japanese forces in ZigZag, opened up with a barrage of artillery that left deep holes in the road, tore up several vehicles, and caused many casualties. A black, nauseous smoke filled the air. Along with fellow troops of the 2nd Battalion, I jumped quickly into the ravine at the side of the road.

Cries for medics permeated intermittent silences. Pfc. Bernard Schneller, the C Company medic, moved up and down the line giving aid whenever needed, pouring Sulfa on wounds, and preparing casualties for evacuation. First Battalion 34th, which had already entered the horseshoe, was hit the hardest: 26 wounded and 13 killed. I joined others to evacuate casualties, which accounted for almost one-third of one platoon. Ambulances churned in relays between the field hospital and the front. Trucks hauled the dead back for military burial.

General Hall had expected the day to be a turning point in the battle. It merely added to his frustrations. The 34th Infantry had been stopped cold.

This was my baptism by fire—my initiation into the hell that was ZigZag Pass.

When our 2nd Battalion reached the turn into the horseshoe, as dusk approached Major Snavely ordered us to dig in for the night alongside Highway 7. We dug foxholes in a circle to accommodate each company, with enlisted men stationed on the perimeter and officers in the center. The captain of my unit—G Company—staked out an area at the top of a hill on the north side of Highway 7. Each platoon divided into groups of three men to a foxhole. My group took small, GI-issue folding spades from our backpacks and dug foxholes about ten inches deep to protect our bodies from horizontal fire and wide enough so that two of us could lie side-by-side to get some rest and, with luck, some sleep, while the third stood guard. We took turns on guard duty—two hours on and four hours off.

It was my lot to be on guard during the last turn before daybreak. It was still pitch dark—but approaching daybreak—when I heard periodic rustling in the nearby bushes. I sensed that an enemy soldier was sneaking toward us. I stiffened, my hands shook, and my mouth went dry. *What should I do? Should I alert my foxhole buddies? What if he tosses a grenade in our direction?* My heart was throbbing so hard I was sure the enemy could hear it. My heartbeat accelerated as rustling sounds indicated that the Jap was drawing closer and closer. As quietly as possible, I flipped open the safety switch on my M-1 rifle and, withholding fire, aimed it in the direction of the sound of what I was sure was the enemy approaching.

As the darkness turned to dawn, I strained my eyes to get a better glimpse. A brown form emerged—something much larger than a human. *What kind of monster is this?* It was a lumbering, docile caribou foraging for its morning meal.

February 4

Just before midnight on February 3, Colonel Jenna informed Major Snavely that the 2nd Battalion's mission the next day was to seize the high ground—a ridgeline overlooking the valley of the Santa Rita River, almost to the "hairpin" loop—1,000 yards east from where we were dug in for the night. The ridgeline appeared to be where the mortar and artillery fire of February 3 had originated. It was impossible to see the enemy. They fired from caves and tunnels and camouflaged holes.

In preparation for the mission, Major Snavely coordinated an all-night artillery barrage, four times as heavy as any so far. The Japanese fired back sporadically.

After the all-night artillery duel, I and members of my platoon shared a hurried breakfast of ten-in-one rations—boxes with enough processed food for ten soldiers for a day. Shortly after daybreak,

Snavely sent patrols to scout the road into the horseshoe and the high ground inside the horseshoe. At about 0800, he led F and G Companies along the hillside of Mount Koko, Major Ogawa's domain. He called forth flamethrowers and three tanks. The commander of one of the tanks found that his .30 caliber machine gun would not silence the Japanese machine guns. He swung his turret in the direction of the Japanese and obliterated that nest with one shot from his 75-mm gun. But that was only one nest.

As the day wore on, our G Company, under command of Captain Rucker G. Innes, trudged single file up the ridge along a twisting jungle trail. I envied the zeal and bravery displayed by suave Second Lieutenant Paul Silber, who had come over with us on the *Howze*, as he led his platoon, though it was not my platoon, along Highway 7 and through the jungle. Lt. Silber was a handsome, though not a tall, man. His confident demeanor made him stand out among his peers. His men obviously respected him and followed his lead.

When we were only a few feet from the top of the ridge, a murderous enemy fire broke loose. F and G Companies had 76 wounded and 12 killed. Word was passed that Lt. Silber had been killed. His chest was split open with an artillery fragment.

> Then came the arduous, heart- and back-breaking labor of carrying the dead and wounded back down the trail. The available litters were soon used up. Many soldiers improvised litters from ponchos and bamboo poles from the thick stands of bamboo in the area. Many able-bodied men served as litter bearers, returning to the scene of the disaster two and three times bearing litters. The lightly wounded assisted the more seriously injured, the walking wounded. Captain Cameron and his medical team did yeoman's work far into the night.[19]

Sixty years later, I was delighted to learn from David Mann's book, *Avenging Bataan*, that Lt. Silber had indeed survived:

> Medical personnel at all levels worked ceaselessly, selflessly, gallantly to succor the never-ending stream of casualties. Chest and fracture cases swamped the 18th PSH (Portable Surgical Hospital) located in the dry rice paddies north of Olongapo. ... Lieutenant Silber of the 2nd Platoon G Company, who survived, had been hit in the chest by a mortar

shell fragment. "You could literally see his heart beating in his chest cavity, and he was alive!" a regimental staff officer commented. …

Six ambulances plied the road all night between the horseshoe and the [two] hospitals. Personnel Carriers, 2 ½-ton trucks, anything that could move, transported the wounded to the clearing stations and hospitals in the rear. Litters, blankets, plasma and bandages moved in a steady stream toward the front.[20]

Even though he was wounded, Capt. Innes, the G Company commander, remained in the area until the last casualty was evacuated. G Company executive officer, Lt. Calhoun, relieved Innes. Presumably to conserve ammunition, the hard-pressed enemy did not interfere further with our 2nd Battalion's removing the dead and wounded.

I helped carry "Red" Hill, my Camp Hood buddy who was one of the wounded in F Company, to an ambulance. I remember his words exactly. He said, "Hesser, I've got 13 holes in me." None appeared to be life threatening, but he was a bloody mess. The medic gave him a shot of morphine and sprinkled sulfa powder on his wounds before applying bandages. "Red" forced a smile when we said goodbye as we loaded him into the ambulance.

We were in no shape to receive yet another attack, so Major Snavely ordered us to move back to defensible ground and dig in. We new replacements soon learned the veterans' routine for digging in while it was still daylight. Battalion troops dug a perimeter of foxholes, three men to a hole. Major Snavely located his command post near the center of the perimeter. Each platoon leader dug in behind his platoon.

As we in G Company started to dig in on a hillside, an enemy soldier with a walkie-talkie, perched high in a tall tree and unnoticed by us as yet, radioed G Company's position to his mortar company. All of a sudden, mortar shells started exploding all around us. The next several minutes—it seemed like hours—were literal hell:

Suddenly, at about 1730, the earth shuddered as a torrent of shells fell savagely on the open, exposed companies. The barrage … sped down the hillside to G Company. There was no warning, no bracketing fire, just ear shattering explosions and buzzing shell fragments, made even more deadly by treetop detonations. The … men hugged the earth and hoped no fragments would find them. …

Many shells exploded in the trees, spreading their zinging fragments over a wide area. Faint cries of "medic, medic," could be heard among pauses in the ear-splitting roar of incoming rounds.[21]

The noise, the stench and the confusion overwhelmed me. Alternately, I buried my face in the ground and prayed, then jumped up and ran for a safer spot. It seemed that each time I ran, a shell exploded where I had been lying. *I shall never doubt that God held my hand.*

Fear is an incredible motivator. I was no longer interested in being a hero. I just wanted to stay alive, and help my buddies stay alive.

I helped evacuate casualties.

One of our old-timers spotted the Japanese radioman high in the tree. With one carefully aimed fire from his Garand, the old vet dropped him.

Just before dark, we regrouped, quickly dug foxholes, and settled in.

The experience that I had in a foxhole on the night of February 3, when I mistook a docile caribou for a marauding Jap on my first night in active combat, was indeed frightening. The night of February 4 was worse. I thought I had met my maker. I was on guard duty, having rotated with the other two men in my foxhole who were now asleep, or at least resting. I was obviously jittery from the day's dreadful experience of mortar shells bursting all around and wounded men screaming for help. All that night, the Japanese fired an occasional mortar in our direction to disturb our rest, as a minimum, and maybe to kill a few. One of the mortars caught a branch of a nearby tree and exploded. A piece of shrapnel came buzzing down through the trees and hit the earth in front of me. I was sure it was a live mortar shell. My mind snapped. I jumped into the adjoining foxhole about two feet away, not realizing that if the mortar had been live, I would already be dead. One of the men there, thinking I was a Japanese soldier in a Bonsai attack, grabbed me tightly and shouted, "I've got him. Stab him!"

I said, "I'm an American! I'm an American!" They didn't believe me. I was so new to the outfit that we scarcely knew each others' names. The three of them held me and asked questions until I finally convinced them that I was one of the new recruits; that in a frightened stupor I had jumped in from the adjoining foxhole.

That experience dealt me a harsh new meaning for the phrase, *I was nearly scared to death!*

Next morning, one of the veterans in the neighboring foxhole told me that he had reached in his boot for his combat knife and was within a fraction of a second of running it through me.

Apparently, I was not the only one to have made the same mistake. Author David Mann reports that on the night of February 1, in ZigZag Pass, a Japanese soldier jumped in a foxhole with two Americans. "One of them, a replacement, panicked and jumped into an adjacent hole. On guard was Guiseppe Ciancarlo … (who) greeted this unfortunate replacement with a chop to his face with a machete! Ciancarlo quickly realized that his victim was a GI and stopped before killing him."[22]

February 5

At about 11:00 p.m. on February 4, Colonel Jenna had orders from above that the next morning the 34th Infantry was to "attack without delay, capture enemy fortified area [about 1,000 yards northeast of the horseshoe and] hold present positions astride Highway 7 and south thereof."[23]

The cooks were awake before sunrise. They lit their field stoves in defiance of snipers. At dawn, along with my mates, I rolled out of my foxhole and apologized for causing such a ruckus during the night. We cursed the damned war. Then, we drank hot coffee and ate a fat mess of dehydrated eggs.

Together with some elements of the 38th Division, our 34th embarked about 0800 on its mission to attack the Japanese. Old-timers in my platoon grumbled about the orders to attack: "Don't the damned Generals know by now what we're up against!"

We continued to advance through wooded mountainsides and passed remnants of abandoned logging camps. Jungle covered the precipices. As the day unfolded, it was the Japanese once again who dominated the battlefield. The enemy's machine guns and mortars cut the air to ribbons and stemmed our advance.

Our 2nd Battalion, still "licking its wounds" from the previous night's bombardment, took the hardest blows. About noon, four Japanese high-explosive rounds plummeted from the brassy sky and hit the trunks of trees over the foxholes of the 2nd Battalion command post, effectively eliminating the operations staff from command.

Together with other members of 2nd Battalion's G Company, I nestled in the ditch beside Highway 7. The ravine echoed the cries of the dying. Once again, I escaped direct harm. When firing ceased, in response to cries for "medics, medics," I joined others to carry litters of dead, near-dead, and seriously wounded to awaiting ambulances and 6x6s.

Among the day's casualties were twelve members of 2nd Battalion aid station, which suffered a direct hit.

Under the blightening horror of the barrage the assault team gave way. The many dead on the highway were torn to bits by a succession of explosions. The wounded lay writhing with jagged holes in their chests or bellies, with an arm or leg shattered, or with broken bones. The day's thousand-yard advance was made for naught.[24]

Another casualty was the BAR man in my squad: shot and killed by an enemy sniper. Only six of the original ten members in the squad were now battle worthy.

All the above, especially the barrage that decimated 2nd Battalion Headquarters, effectively rendered the battalion incapable of further offensive action. When Colonel Jenna learned the condition of his leading battalions, he fired off a message to General Jones:

I AM CONVINCED THAT THE ENTIRE JAP POSITION OPPOSING XI CORPS CANNOT BE CRACKED UNLESS THERE IS A WITHDRAWAL TO A POINT WHERE ENTIRE CORPS ARTY AND ALL AVAILABLE AIR WORKS IT OVER WITH EVERY POSSIBLE MEANS FOR AT LEAST 48 HOURS. MY 1ST AND 2ND BNS HAVE SUFFERED TERRIFIC CASUALTIES, AND IT IS BECOMING QUESTIONABLE HOW LONG THEY CAN HOLD UNDER THIS POUNDING. REQUEST CORPS BE NOTIFIED OF CONTENTS OF THIS MESSAGE.[25]

Colonel Jenna ordered the 2nd Battalion to withdraw to a position about ¼ mile west of the horseshoe, beside Highway 7, where we dug in for the night.

General Hall finally understood what his troops were facing. He reported to General Kruger:

> I have been hard to convince, but now there is no doubt in my mind about being up against a well-defended Jap position. ... The resistance has been extremely strong for the last two days. The enemy has obviously sited and registered his automatic weapons and artillery on every road bend and all commanding ground in this area. ... It is a tough nut to crack. ... It is the best fortified place I have ever seen.[26]

February 6

Early in the morning of February 6, sixteen P-47 Thunderbolts started bombing ZigZag. They employed four tons of bombs, 3,960 gallons of fiery napalm and 63,000 rounds of .50-caliber ammunition. Heavy artillery bombardment supplemented the air strike. This day finally started tipping the scales in favor of the Americans. The aerial bombing and artillery barrage continued for three more days. Two days after that, the 38th Division was able to move through the Pass and on to Dinalupihan.

On February 6, Colonel Jenna received authority to begin moving the battle-weary 34th back down Highway 7 to Subic Bay, near where we had landed on January 29, removing the regiment from further action in ZigZag Pass. By late afternoon, we were in bivouac. Each of us was hot, tired, mad and bewildered by the hard-hitting resistance we had met in ZigZag Pass, but grateful to be alive. There was a lot of grumbling in the ranks, especially among the seasoned vets, about the top echelon's having misjudged the strength of the enemy in ZigZag.

"Doc" Cameron, 2nd Battalion Surgeon, made sure we started our recuperation in style. Defying strict orders, he provided each of us that night with a cocktail of grapefruit juice and 100-proof alcohol![27]

Compared with its other battles, the 34th Infantry Regiment suffered enormous casualties during its short stay in ZigZag Pass. In three days in the Pass, the 34th had 319 casualties, almost half as many as the 748 lost in the 75-day Leyte campaign. In addition were at least 25 cases of severe psychoneurosis, or shell shock. The rifle companies bore the brunt. New replacements made up 40 percent of the casualties, the same percentage as we replacements were in the total strength of the regiment.

"Doc" Cameron summed up the plight of the dazed, bewildered replacements, strangers to the veterans and to each other, suddenly thrust into a terrifying battle in a strange land: "The ZigZag was the only time I ever saw an American soldier break down emotionally. These wounded kids were coming in crying and when I asked them what unit they were from they said, 'I don't know—maybe ? Company.'"[28]

Rest for the Weary

During the next few days, we cleaned our weapons, washed our clothes, bathed in a near-by stream for the first time since landing on Luzon ten days earlier, and rested. We also had a much-appreciated mail call. I had several letters from Florence, who wrote a V-Mail letter to me almost every day. I also had a letter from my mother who said, "Son, if you can get your hands on a Bible, you might find comfort in reading the 91st Psalm."

Several of us, especially some of us newer recruits, carried a miniature New Testament. Mine, presented to me before I left for the Army by the Sunday School Superintendent in the little rural, Congregational Christian church in which I had grown up, had a bronze cover. I carried the New Testament in my left breast pocket "to stop a bullet from penetrating your heart." But, none of us carried a complete Bible, which included the Old Testament. That was excess baggage in jungle warfare.

Early on Sunday, February 11, the Regimental Chaplain announced to the troops that he would hold a worship service later that morning. Filipinos had created a veritable "chapel" in the palm grove next to our camp by placing a series of coconut logs, in parallel fashion, to serve as pews. The service was well attended that Sunday morning—standing room only. The chaplain led us in a couple of familiar hymns. He offered a prayer for those who were killed or wounded in ZigZag. Then, he said, "For my text this morning, I will read from the 91st Psalm."

I knew that Mother was tuned in, but I hadn't realized before that she had a hot line. My eyes watered as the chaplain read the passage:

You will not fear the terror of the night, nor the arrow that flies by day, nor the pestilence that stalks in darkness, nor the destruction that wastes at noonday.

A thousand may fall at your side, ten thousand at your right hand, but it will not come near you. ... For he will give his angels charge of you to guard you in all your ways.

Even some of the old vets had tears in their eyes.

Leon Hesser

Chapter 6: A Medic in Training

After we had been in camp near Subic Bay for a couple of days, my squad leader (I do not remember his name) faced the dilemma of what to do about the loss of his BAR man to a sniper in ZigZag. He said to me, "Hesser, you look strong. How about if you take the BAR?" While I was not terribly excited by that prospect—by now I realized that any man carrying a BAR was a prime target for snipers— I was not one to say, "Better give it to someone else."

Obediently, I took the imposing thing to a makeshift range near the camp and tried it out, to get a feel for it. From a prone position, I fired several clips using the bipod. I shot a few more clips while standing, firing from the hip, using it like a Tommy gun, which was the usual method in jungle fighting. I was duly impressed with the weapon's firepower. At 19 pounds, it was twice as heavy as my Garand, but I thought I could manage it.

As I was returning to camp, a jeep carrying a medical officer, Captain Fremont P. Koch, M.D., pulled up beside me. The captain said, "Is your name Hesser?"

"Yes, sir."

"As you may be aware, we lost some medics during a mortar barrage in ZigZag. I'm looking for a few good men whom we might transfer to re-staff our 2nd Battalion aid station. I would like for you to join us. Would you be interested?"

I said, "Sir, anything is better than carrying this BAR!"

I finished out the war as a medic, being one of the few teenagers during World War II who was awarded both the Combat Infantry Badge and the Combat Medic Badge.

A few months later on Mindanao, I wrote out the tag of a contemporary GI to whom the squad leader had given my BAR: "KIA" (Killed in Action). He was shot by a sniper. I might not have been in the same spot where he was at the time, but I have thought about his fate thousands of times.

Medic Training

About a week after we had bivouacked near Subic Bay, I boarded a Navy ship that took us to Mindoro, a medium sized island just south of Luzon. Mindoro had been invaded earlier by American troops and, except for some Japanese stragglers and the need for some

67

mopping up operations, it was relatively secure. The 34th would take on new replacements and soon be joined by the other two regiments—the 19th and the 21st—of the 24th Infantry Division.

Training for us newly recruited medics started shortly after we settled on Mindoro.

At age 25, Captain Koch was only six years older than I. He had just finished med school. He had been recruited and sent to the Pacific before doing his residency. He was a superb teacher and respected leader.

In a few weeks, we learned the basics of how, under battlefield conditions, to apply tourniquets; give blood transfusions; sprinkle powdered sulfa to open wounds; and how, under what conditions, and in what doses to give morphine shots.

Hesser listening to Pfc Tommy Davis' heartbeat

Doc Koch gave us a brief history for two of the newer, almost miracle medications—sulfa and penicillin—to prevent bacterial infection from wounds. He said that during World War I, doctors could do little more for the wounded than they could have for Stonewall Jackson, who survived surgery for injuries during the Civil War, but died eight days later from wound infection. But the discovery during the late 1930s and early 1940s of sulfa, short for sulfanilamide, proved to be invaluable for its ability to prevent bacterial infections. It was safe and easy to apply. We were each issued a first aid kit containing sulfa and were shown how to sprinkle the powder on any open wound. Capt. Koch said, "If sulfa had been available during the Civil War, Stonewall Jackson and thousands of other soldiers would have survived."

Doc Koch was really excited about the recent discovery and use of penicillin. In 1939 at Oxford University, an Austrian scientist and a team of researchers had made significant progress in showing the bactericidal action of penicillin. It was first successfully used to treat a patient for bacterial infection in 1942, while Koch was in Med school. In 1943, the required clinical trials were performed and penicillin was shown to be the most effective antibacterial agent to date. Availability was severely limited due to the difficulty of manufacturing large quantities, but we on the war front were given priority. Doc explained that penicillin was equally effective as a cure for gonorrhea as it was for wound infections.

Doc Koch spent a lot of time explaining the proper use of morphine as a pain killer. He explained that morphine is processed from the opium poppy plant which was grown in much of Asia. He said that before the American Civil War, opium was either swallowed, taken with a beverage, or smoked. Serious addiction problems often resulted. At the time of the Civil War, the hypodermic syringe was invented. Using the syringe to inject morphine into the blood proved indispensable for patients undergoing surgery.

For use during World War II, a pharmaceutical company developed a morphine syrette as an easy way for medics to administer on the front lines a controlled amount of the drug to wounded soldiers. Doc cautioned that once we had applied the drug, we should pin the syrette to the collar of the casualty. This would serve as a precaution to prevent overdosing of unconscious patients.

At sick call, after a bit of training, we new medics doled out medications at the direction of Doc Koch.

Without preventive treatment, malaria reached epidemic proportions and was debilitating to Army forces in the tropics of the South Pacific. Among the routine treatments for malaria was Atabrine, a substitute for quinine. When the Japanese took control of the Dutch East Indies (Indonesia) in early 1942, they cut off the rest of the world's supply of quinine, which had been harvested for hundreds of years from the bark of the cinchona tree.

As a synthetic anti-malarial drug, Atabrine was developed in the 1930s. Atabrine was a deterrent, but not a surefire control, against malaria. Each GI was to take one of the yellow pills each day. They were bitter. Not all soldiers would take them voluntarily. We medics were frequently posted at the head of mess lines to make sure the men would take the little yellow devils.

After we new recruits had taken the pills for about a month, our skin began to take on a yellow hue. That together with a good suntan and dirty combat boots meant that we were no longer so visibly distinguishable from the old-timers.

Another routine treatment were Halazone tablets, to "purify" our drinking water, which was often taken from rivers and streams. And with each canteen of water, we added a salt pill to replace some of the minerals that our bodies lost from the heavy perspiration that we experienced in the tropics.

One of our routines, when battlefield conditions warranted, was to have men in the Battalion—about 50 at a time—line up and get their periodic typhoid, tetanus, cholera, and diphtheria shots. We did not have throwaway needles at that time, so we kept one man busy boiling needles before they were re-used.

Shortly after we had arrived on Mindoro for the two months of training, Doc Koch's clerk had enough points to rotate back to the States for some well-earned leave. Capt. Koch asked me to be his clerk, which entailed my following him as he met with patients, to transcribe the diagnoses and treatments as he dictated them. With this, I was promoted to corporal. My Army pay went from $55 per month to $60.

Wartime Pastimes

Once each month, Doc Koch was issued a fifth of Bourbon, for medicinal purposes. At least for the two months while we were on Mindoro, facing little or no action, the good doctor shared the Bourbon with his team—about one ounce for each of us, once a month. That was my introduction to hard liquor. Drinking age in Indiana was 21, but in the war-zone, no one asked to see my ID.

During the two months on Mindoro we had time for recreation. Different units formed teams and played others in "intramural" volleyball, softball, and basketball. Our team was dubbed the "2nd Battalion Pill Rollers.

Hesser's serve in a game of badmington

Another favorite pastime was the card game, pinochle, which we usually played at night. Two of us would combine our pup tents into a larger one and then invite two buddies to join in a foursome. A flashlight wedged in the top of the tent provided sufficient light. We didn't bet; the game was strictly to pass the time. Even so, my mother would not have approved!

The tents of commissioned officers were, of course, larger than those for us enlisted men. I remember a well-placed, hand-painted sign outside Captain Koch's tent which read, "Bedside Manor."

While we were on Mindoro, we were blessed with regular mail calls. Among the most memorable letters that I received during that time was one from Florence. I was puzzled when it started out, "Dear Bob." It seems that she had written letters to both me and her cousin Bob Critten, an officer in the Navy, and sent each of them in the envelope intended for the other. Bob got the love letter intended for me and I received the letter meant for Bob. It was indeed revealing; it provided insight about the family's none-too-happy reaction to Florence's being engaged to a "farm boy." After the war, Bob assured me from the message in Florence's love letter that I had nothing to worry about!

Shortly after we arrived on Mindoro, we were told that on February 19 the Marines had invaded Iwo Jima, a strategic island guarding the flight path to Japan. The tiny atoll would serve as a base for our B-29 Superfortresses; the distance of B-29 raids would be nearly halved. It would serve as a staging area for the eventual invasion of the Japanese Home Islands. And it would deny the Japanese the ability to use the island as an airbase for their aircraft to intercept our long-range bombers.

The bad news, which we would learn much later, was that

Iwo Jima was a hard-won victory. The 37-day battle was one of the bloodiest of the Pacific war. Nearly a third of the 80,000 American troops who fought there, mostly Marines, were killed or wounded. Of the 22,000 Japanese defenders, about 21,000 died.

While on Mindoro, we were saddened to learn that President Franklin Delano Roosevelt had died of a massive stroke on April 12, 1945. Vice President Harry S. Truman became President.

Several of us said, "Harry who??" Mr. Truman had been Vice President for only a short three months. I wondered, *What is his perspective as Commander in Chief?*

Chapter 7: Four Months on Mindanao

On April 13, 1945, the 24th Division, which included the 19th and 21st Infantry Regiments in addition to the 34th, set sail from Mindoro for Mindanao, the southernmost and second largest island of the Philippines. The objective was to re-take Davao, the country's second largest city after Manila, on Davao Gulf on the east side of the island.

In the 1930s, thousands of Japanese had settled in the Philippines. The city of Davao had been a hub of Japanese colonization. After the fall of Manila, Davao was the last major stronghold of the Japanese military in the Philippine archipelago. The bulk of some 50,000 Japanese troops defending Mindanao were encamped in the Province of Davao.

The massive guns of the Japanese all pointed east, toward Davao Gulf, where they expected the Americans to invade. Knowing this, General MacArthur ordered the 100-ship convoy of the Allied forces to Parang, in Moro Gulf, on the west side of the island. The beach was narrow, black, and steep where we made a beachhead on April 17. The Japanese were not expecting us to land on the more rugged west coast, so the landing was unopposed.

While exploring Parang, one of our soldiers found a crumpled cage with five carrier pigeons. Two had been killed in the preparatory barrage. Three were alive. All of them had messages attached to their legs: "The Americans are here." The GI removed the messages to keep as a souvenir.

An amphibious reconnaissance group, after exploring the gloomy estuary of the Mindanao River, sent back word that they had seen many crocodiles but no Japs. I thought, *If we have to wade across rivers, which will be the most dangerous?*

The first day, because the Japanese had burned a 240-foot bridge across the Ambal River, we waded across, shoulder deep, holding high our weapons and ammunition. Fortunately, we saw no crocs.

The "National Highway" from Parang to Davao was mostly a one-lane track with hundreds of twisting curves through half-explored wilderness—broad valleys, high mountains, belts of jungle, and more than 50 rivers and streams. The road, long unused, twisted through a dark jungle of immense trees, ravines, cliffs, tangled stream beds and inscrutable mountain sides. The sun blazed. During the first two or three days as we marched down the jungle road, cases of heat exhaustion plagued scores of our troops.

The Japanese had destroyed most of the bridges. Our Engineers replaced some of them with pontoon bridges. We marched most of the way, but took our turn in 6x6 trucks when they were available. Mostly on foot, we stormed the 150 miles from Parang to Davao in two hectic weeks.

The code name for the 34th Infantry Regiment was "Dragon." The three battalions were "Red," "White," and "Blue." Communication between 2nd Battalion and 1st Battalion, with walkie-talkie radios, would go something like this: "Dragon Red, this is Dragon White; Dragon Red, this is Dragon White; Over." First Battalion would then respond with, "Dragon White, this is Dragon Red; Dragon White, this is Dragon Red; Over." Their conversation would then continue, advising each other what they observed and cautioning what to watch for.

After about the first week of marching across Mindanao, carrying full gear, we weary troops began saying to each other, "Dragon White, this is draggin' ass; Dragon White, this is draggin' ass." A bit of levity helped ease the monotony and pain.

The weather—rain, rain, rain—was a constant adverse factor. We troops could seldom get dry. Several times, in my foxhole at night, I took off a boot to use for a pillow, to keep my head above water inside the foxhole. Along with most of the others, I had "jungle rot," an itchy rash on the feet and legs, caused by dampness and a shortage of dry socks.

Much of Mindanao, about the size of Indiana, was marked "unexplored" on maps. The people were different from the friendly Filipinos we had met on Luzon. On a few occasions, from a distance, we saw small groups of the proud and never-conquered Muslim Moros, who average slightly over 5 feet in height, peering at us frombehind bushes in the jungle. Moro guerillas had a reputation as keen warriors who were deadly with a blowgun and poison darts. They were a fierce and volatile people who practiced polygamy, slavery and rape of infidels. They were proud, untamed, and self confident. Even with our modern and superior war machines, I hoped they would keep their distance. They did.

As we approached Davao District, word passed that other tribes on the island still practiced head hunting and cannibalism, and that they had a reputation for treating Japanese, Americans and Filipinos alike.[b] Among the other tribes were the Manobos. They were described to us as wild, pagan tree dwellers with long hair, and whose teeth were filed flat. The Bagobos were a primitive tribe who lived in the unexplored hinterland of Davao Province. The Negritos were said to be small, pitch black, with broad heads and thick lips, who were commonly armed with blow-pipes to shoot poisoned arrows.

Fortunately, I never came face to face with any of those natives, but the thought of them lurking behind trees as we traversed the jungle was always on my mind. Truth is, the remaining "head hunter" tribes in the Philippines were isolated in the extreme northern part of Luzon, not on Mindanao.

Among the more pleasant sights on Mindanao was the greenery—the foliage. The mountainsides were covered with forests of towering teak, ironwood, cypress, ebony and other tropical species that fascinated this Indiana farm boy.

Japanese resistance became stronger as we drew closer to Davao, and our pace slowed. Whenever we came to any substantial resistance, our commander would pull us back about 100 yards and call in the Navy dive-bombers. I marveled at the grace and precision of these fly-guys as they piloted their Curtiss Helldivers. They would dive almost straight down toward a target, release a bomb, and immediately pull up. The roar and the power of the planes' gasoline engines as they pulled out of the dive gave us dogfaces a chill. In most instances, then, we could walk right through.

One time we were close enough to Japanese soldiers that we could hear them talking to each other. We took cover in ditches beside the road when they began lobbing mortar shells. Luckily, most of the mortars went over our heads and beyond. I laughed almost

---

b   Earlier in the 20th century, anthropologists from the Field Museum of Natural History had studied the Bagobo, Kulaman, Mandaya, and a couple of other tribes of Davao District and reported in *The Wild Tribes of Davao District, Mindanao,* that "In each tribe the warriors gain distinction among their fellows ... by killing a certain number of persons. ... While it is true that the Kulaman take the heads ... of slain foes, and that the same custom is some times followed by individual warriors of other tribes, head-hunting for the sake of the trophy is not practiced here, as is the case in Northern Luzon."

hysterically at my buddy Neal Burwell, who kept running from one place to another, obviously scared stiff, trying to find the safest haven. The fact that I could laugh in the face of such danger indicated to me that I had matured substantially since the Battle of ZigZag Pass. I was now a veteran.

Still, most events were not laughing matters. It was on Mindanao that I wrote out the tag for the man who was given my BAR when I transferred to the Medics: "KIA." A sniper had shot him in the back.

A few days later, in a hot skirmish in an open space in the jungle, a Camp Hood mate who had come over with me on the USS *General Howze* was killed. Let's say his name was Mike. Because of the gruesome story, and the effect it might have on his family if they know about it, I prefer not to use his real name.

As the company's soldiers retreated in haste, they were unable to bring out Mike's body, which lay exposed in the sweltering sun. Three days later, when it was deemed safe to re-enter the area, I volunteered along with three other 2nd Battalion medics to rescue Mike's grotesquely deteriorated and swollen body. The only way we could accurately identify him was by his dog tag. The odor was so strong we could hardly breathe. We stood back, took deep breaths, ran toward the body, threw a poncho over it and, as gently as possible, lifted it onto the litter.

On the way back to camp, we had to pass through "Caribou Gulch," a valley that was littered with the corpses of a score of dead Japanese and a dozen caribou that were killed in the artillery barrage three days earlier. The stench of Caribou Gulch combined with that of Mike's body was so overpowering that it affected me psychologically. For many months after the war, I had no sense of smell. I was unable to detect odors as pungent as those of a skunk. Even today, when I get a whiff of a disagreeable odor, it brings to mind that gut-wrenching experience.

On April 22, we passed through the town of Kabukan, which sits at the cross roads of the east-west and the north-south highways of central Mindanao. On April 24, we reached Saguing, about 30 miles from Davao Gulf. As we approached Davao, the Japanese had mined the roads with hundreds of aerial bombs. Since they no longer had planes, they had found other uses for their aerial bombs. They buried them so that only about an inch of their noses showed above ground. Wires attached to the detonating mechanism led to foxholes 40 to 50 yards into the jungle. A Jap sitting in a foxhole, with the tug of a wire, could set off a violent explosion.

Our Army engineers had discovered and disarmed many of the bombs, but not all of them. On April 27, as we entered Digos Town, not far from the Gulf of Davao, the road was heavily mined. Pfc. Handy, another *General Howze* buddy, died instantly from the explosion of one of these bombs. One leg was severed, just below the hip. Almost as a routine, I picked up the pieces, placed them on a litter, and wrote out his tag: "KIA."

On April 28—after a twelve-hour battle—we of the 34th Infantry Regiment were the first to see the "glittering blue of the ocean," the first to cross Mindanao Island from coast to coast. Several miles to the north lay the city of Davao.[29] On May 2, one of the other regiments of the 24th Division punched into Davao City. Our 34th Regiment followed.

A few days later, word was passed that Germany had surrendered. I was grateful. America's full attention could now be aimed at the Pacific theater.

For the next three months, the Japanese fought with arrogance, with a complete contempt for death. Bonsai attacks were frequent. They apparently were following strict orders passed down by the hard-line military leaders: to surrender would be worse than death.

The 24th Division's field artillery, aiming at enemy positions, thundered day and night. Dive bombers dropped Napalm and high-explosive bombs. Fanning out from Davao, every battalion of every regiment was in continuous battle. Valtin reports that "the men of the Twenty-Fourth Infantry Division were locked in the hardest, bitterest, most exhausting battle of their ten island campaigns. ... More than ten thousand Japanese died around Davao at the hands of Twenty-Fourth Division men."[30]

Nature also took its toll. Heat prostrations resulted from the sweltering sky and earth, day after day. And unfortunate accidents were more common than one would like to think. Some of the first Americans to die in this, the last campaign of the Philippine war, were victims of accidents:

> One night a green replacement crawled out of his foxhole to pee. A soldier in the neighboring hole saw movement in the dark and shot him dead.
>
> [On another occasion] a soldier thought he heard a noise

in a clump of bushes. He tossed a grenade. The grenade struck a palm trunk and bounced back into the thrower's foxhole, where it exploded and killed him.[31]

In the European theater during the war, a medic usually wore a red cross and carried no weapon. That system was not honored in the Pacific; from the Japanese perspective, medics were legitimate targets. So, we carried weapons. But, rather than a 9-pound Garand rifle and bayonet, we Pill Rollers were issued much-lighter carbines. Most of us also had .45 caliber pistols. Especially when carrying a litter with a casualty, we left the carbine behind and took the easier to carry though less accurate .45.

Each of 2nd Battalion's four rifle companies had a trained medic who stayed with his assigned company. When one of the companies had casualties, we 2nd Battalion Pill Rollers were called forward to assist the company medic care for the wounded and then, for those who were unable to walk, to carry them on a litter back to the aid station where Doc Koch would handle the case.

One day when one of 2nd Battalion's companies was hit hard, four of us Pill Rollers went forward to help the company's medic treat wounded and then carry out the dead and those wounded who were unable to walk. The company commander dispatched eight of his infantrymen to carry litters with two dead soldiers while we four medics carried back to the aid station a badly wounded corporal. He had taken a piece of shrapnel in the gut. It was a long trek, half a mile or more, on a muddy trail through the jungle.

Before we picked up the corporal, the company medic had administered blood plasma. We had gone a few hundred yards when we noticed that the soldier's complexion had turned white. His vital signs were weak, at best. We panicked. I said, "Let's give him some more blood." We paused in a secluded area and tried. Two of us tried to inject plasma, one in each arm, to no avail. While we were still in training, Doc Koch had told us that if veins in the arms collapsed, to try injecting the plasma in a prominent vein in the penis. I tried that. It didn't work. The young man had died. When we arrived back at the aid station, Doc Koch said we had done all we could have under the circumstances. The corporal's wound was too severe.

The first time I saw a buddy die, in ZigZag Pass, it was horrible. Words cannot describe the feeling. I'm sorry to say, though, I was starting to get used to it. During the twelve months since I was inducted into Uncle Sam's Army, I had been transformed from an innocent, naive, invincible Indiana farm boy to a battle-hardened soldier who took death and bloodshed in stride. Well, almost. As a teenager, I had seen more blood and death than I care to remember.

By my 20th birthday, on July 27, I felt more like a 30-year-old. Ironically, as an octogenarian I now feel more like 50 or 60.

Just before I turned 20, I was promoted to buck sergeant to take the place of one of the old-timers who had accumulated enough points to rotate back to the states for home leave. I forget Sarg's name, but he was an unforgettable character. At times when we were not in the midst of battle, he would take a stethoscope and go trotting off to a village where he would pose as a doctor. Especially for young women, he would disseminate a handful of Atabrine tablets to relieve their malaria symptoms, but only after using his "tityscope" to examine their chests. We all laughed at his antics, although it seemed to some of us to be morally inappropriate. If officers knew about it, they apparently didn't admonish him. They had bigger problems to deal with.

A devastating type of malaria was endemic on Mindanao. Atabrine helped relieve the symptoms, but was certainly not a cure. During the summer of 1945, I came down with a bad case of the chills and was dispatched to a field hospital where they treated me with quinine, a more effective medication, but one that was in such short supply that it was not doled out routinely. After about ten days, the quinine had effectively contained the malady and I was back on duty. However, for two or three years after the war, periodically I came down with malaria, which demonstrated itself with a case of chills every other day for several days.

One day I was one of six medics who accompanied Doc Koch on a mission to take care of a Japanese soldier who was reported to be alone, listless, and of no threat militarily. When we found him, he appeared to be "bombed out" either from self-medicated dope, or near death from some disease. To put the man out of his misery, Doc Koch suggested that each of us give him a generous shot of morphine, as an act of mercy. In turn, we each administered a shot. Since it was done collectively no one of us would need to feel morally responsible for the man's death. I still think about it. I wish I hadn't done it.

Doc Koch, whom we all admired, had married his sweetheart, Eunice, just shortly before he boarded a ship for the Philippines. On one of our periodic baths in a river, in which we stripped off all our clothes and washed them at the same time we took a bath, several of us medics had a laugh and a good taste of the Captain's feelings toward his new wife: from one of the oversize pockets of his fatigues, he pulled out a brassiere and washed it. He had been carrying the brassiere and, presumably, its sentiments for months.

Plans for Invading Japan

When the fall of Saipan in July 1944 brought U.S. bombers within range of Tokyo, Prime Minister Hideki Tojo, who had ordered the December 7, 1941 attack on Pearl Harbor, resigned. It was becoming evident that Japan was losing the war. But there were problems with breaking the news to the Japanese people, who had been told only of victories. Japan's generals were determined to continue the war. Allied insistence on unconditional surrender provided an excuse for their continuing to fight.

In August 1944, during the time that I was in training at Camp Hood, Admiral Nimitz and General MacArthur were developing secret plans to invade the Philippines later that year. They were also developing plans to invade Japan. They and the Joint Chiefs of Staff in Washington, DC, saw little hope that the country's leaders would surrender unconditionally without an invasion of their Home Islands.

By early autumn of 1944, U.S. military planners generally agreed that aerial bombing and naval blockade would not force Japan's surrender. Immense invasions would be needed, first of Kyushu and then of Honshu, the two main islands. They tentatively set the first operation for November 1945 and the second for early 1946. Pentagon officials and field commanders knew those assaults would be difficult and would produce high American casualties.

After the Battle of Leyte Gulf in October 1944, with Japan's catastrophic loss of ships and men, and with American subs routinely sinking Japanese ships carrying oil and other strategic materials, there was no way that Japan could keep pace with America's ability to turn out ships, tanks, planes, weapons and fighting men and women. But Army Intelligence indicated that the Japanese leaders were determined to fight to the last.

History records that in early 1945, Emperor Hirohito began a series of individual meetings with senior government officials. All but one advised continuing the war. The exception, ex-Prime Minister Konoe, urged a negotiated surrender. The Emperor took the view that peace was both desirable and essential, but that the armed forces would have to have a significant military victory someplace, to provide a stronger bargaining position. As the weeks passed, such a victory became less likely. In April, the Soviet Union advised Japan that it would not renew its neutrality agreement. Japan's ally Germany surrendered in early May. In June, Japan's cabinet decided more firmly than ever to fight to the last man. Extremists called for death-before-dishonor—mass suicide.

After German troops surrendered unconditionally to Allied forces, the complete attention of Allied forces could now be directed toward the Japanese. Japan's leaders saw the inevitable. Sooner or later, their Home Islands would be invaded.

We suspected while we were in training, and history was later to confirm, that the Japanese people were being told that the entire nation will fight to the very end rather than accept unconditional surrender. The widely distributed *Peoples' Handbook* gave instructions to Japan's civilians on how they should fight with sticks, stones, or any weapons that they could muster.

The Joint Chiefs of Staff had decided that, after Iwo Jima, the island of Okinawa, which the Japanese had invaded centuries earlier and claimed as theirs, would be next. The island would serve as the major staging area for invading the Japanese homelands.

The Battle of Okinawa was the largest amphibious assault of the Pacific campaigns. Total Allied strength was 548,000 regulars: Army, Navy and Marines. The battle lasted from April 1 to June 21, 1945. It confirmed that the Japanese would not give up easily. At least 122,000 Japanese civilians, about one-third of the civilian population, in addition to 66,000 Japanese military personnel, were killed in the battle; 17,000 were wounded. Many soldiers simply blew themselves up with grenades.

The Japanese involved more than 1,500 planes in *kamikaze* (suicide) attacks. Of the Allied fleet of 1,300 ships, nearly a score were sunk; many others were damaged. The U.S. Navy had more casualties at Okinawa than anywhere else in the war.

Some of the large Okinawa civilian population, convinced by Japanese propaganda that American soldiers were barbarians who committed horrible atrocities, killed their families and themselves to avoid capture. Many Okinawans threw themselves and family members to their deaths from cliffs; others were murdered by Japanese to avoid their capture.

Allied forces paid a heavy price for Okinawa: 12,513 dead or missing and 38,916 wounded. Winston Churchill called the battle among the most intense and famous in military history. Although Okinawa turned out to be the last major battle of the war, neither side expected the fighting to end there—the Home Islands of Japan would have to be invaded.

On May 20, the Japanese began withdrawing from China. Their troops were needed to defend the homeland. They were preparing for the expected invasion.

After the Japanese lost Okinawa in June 1945, their strategy was to inflict a serious blow to the U.S. forces when they invaded Japan and then to make a peace proposal. Japanese leaders hoped that an armistice or peace with the U.S. would follow the Battle of the Homeland.

Following the Allied occupation of Okinawa, the U.S. prepared military plans to invade the island of Kyushu and the Kanto Plain, which includes Tokyo, on the island of Honshu. General MacArthur was designated ground commander for the invasion. America's strategy was to force Japan into an unconditional surrender.

It was well-known that the Japanese would resist with all their might. Their military leaders planned to station 250,000 troops on Kyushu, the southernmost of Japan's four main islands, where they would counter-attack with 6,000 *kamikaze* aircraft. The suicidal missions would attempt to destroy a quarter of Allied invasion forces before they landed, while they were still aboard their amphibious troop carriers.

We in the 24th Division, while in the province of Davao, were being prepared psychologically and militarily for the invasion of Japan's homelands. I could not begin to comprehend what such an invasion would be like. I was not alone. We were all frightened.

Surrender or Face Destruction

The Potsdam Conference in Germany, from July 17 to August 2, 1945, was mainly on how to administer the defeated Nazi Germany, which had agreed to unconditional surrender on May 8. Future moves in the war against Japan were also on the agenda. On July 16, while on his way to Potsdam, President Harry S. Truman was informed that the first A-bomb test, the "Trinity," at a site in the desert near Alamogordo, New Mexico, was a success.

On July 26, the Potsdam Declaration, or the Proclamation Defining Terms of Japanese Surrender, was issued by President Truman, Prime Minister Winston Churchill, and China's Chiang

Kai-Shek, outlining the terms of surrender for Japan as agreed at the Potsdam Conference.

Coincidentally, on my 20th birthday, July 27, the Allied powers requested Japan, as outlined in the Potsdam Declaration, to surrender or face destruction. The proclamation stated that the full force of the United States, the British Empire, and China would strike the final blows upon Japan. They warned that the power of the Allies would lead to "the inevitable and complete destruction of the Japanese armed forces and just as inevitably the utter devastation of the Japanese homeland" unless Japan ended the war.

In the Potsdam declaration, the United States had changed its strategy from "unconditional surrender" to "unconditional surrender of the armed forces of Japan." That subtle change caused Emperor Hirohito to take a stronger position against the hardliners, to strive somehow to end the war.

The Potsdam Declaration also stated that:

- Militarism in Japan must end;
- Japan would be occupied until the basic objectives set out in this proclamation were met;
- Japanese sovereignty would be limited to the islands of Honshu, Hokkaido, Kyushu, Shikoku and such minor islands as the Allies determined;
- Japanese army would be completely disarmed and allowed to return home;
- Those who had led Japan to war must be permanently and finally discredited, and abandoned;
- War criminals would be punished including those who had "visited cruelties upon our prisoners." Freedom of speech, of religion, and of thought, as well as respect for the fundamental human rights shall be established;
- Japan should be permitted to maintain a viable industrial economy but not industries which would enable her to re-arm for war;
- The treaty was not intended to enslave Japanese as a race or as a nation;
- Allied forces would be withdrawn from Japan as soon as these objectives have been accomplished.[32]

Just four days after the conclusion of the Potsdam Conference, on August 6 the A-bomb was dropped over Hiroshima. I can't begin to explain the reaction I had when we were told the news. I was stunned. I felt nauseous. The magnitude of the destructive force of the A-bomb was incomprehensible to me. I thought surely that this would cause the Japanese leaders to realize the futility of continuing their struggle. It *must* mean that the end of the war was near and that I would be going home. At that prospect, I was elated. At the same time, I was terribly disturbed by the thought of the immense power of this new destructive device.

Compared with the nuclear weapons of the 21st century, with 100 times the force of "Little Boy" that was dropped over Hiroshima, the A-bomb was a firecracker.

Chapter 8: The A-Bomb and Hiroshima

When President Roosevelt died suddenly on April 12, 1945, Vice President Harry Truman had not yet been told about the atomic bomb, which at that time was nearing completion. Within 24 hours of Roosevelt's death, Secretary of War Henry Stimson told President Truman about the bomb. The new President would receive a more extensive briefing on April 25.

Early in 1939 several physicists, mostly Europeans, concluded that when atoms of a certain isotope of uranium are bombarded with neutrons, they split, releasing energy and more neutrons. The discovery raised the possibility of staging an energy-releasing chain reaction, with explosive power never before known. Many scientists were alarmed that an enormously destructive weapon based on this discovery might first be developed by Nazi Germany.

In August 1939, three Hungarian physicists, Leo Szilard, Eugene Wigner, and Edward Teller, who had fled to the United States from the Nazi threat, went to see Albert Einstein, the doyen of the scientific community, and persuaded him to write to President Roosevelt to warn him that a nuclear bomb might be under development in Germany. Einstein alerted the President, who authorized the formation of a scientific committee to study whether a nuclear weapon was feasible. Following the strong recommendation of scientists, who were convinced that their German rivals had a two-year head start, Roosevelt approved a crash program to build atomic bombs.[33]

In June 1941, Roosevelt established "the Manhattan Project" and tasked it with designing and building the first atomic bomb. Leslie R. Groves, who had managed the building of the Pentagon in Washington, DC, was appointed to direct the project. The top-secret project involved teams of scientists working on separate problems at several locations throughout the United States. The making of the atomic bomb, which involved more than 600,000 people, was by far the most sophisticated large-scale effort ever made by man.

At his briefing on April 25, 1945, President Truman was told that enough plutonium-235 material for an implosion assembly would be tested in early July. A second assembly of plutonium-235 would be ready in August. Sufficient uranium-235, with potentially more destructive capacity than that from plutonium-235, would be available around August 1. Several B-29s had been modified to carry the weapons, and construction was underway at Tinian, in the Mariana Islands, about 1,500 miles south of Japan, to support and launch planes to carry the bombs.

Under the direction of physicist J. Robert Oppenheimer, researchers at Los Alamos, New Mexico, successfully tested the first atomic bomb on July 16, 1945. The test bomb, named Trinity, was an implosion-type, based on plutonium fuel. It had a yield of 21 kilotons (equivalent to 21,000 tons of TNT).[34]

President Truman, with the trademark sign on his Oval Office desk that said, "The Buck Stops Here," was weighing the pros and cons of authorizing use of the weapon as a means of potentially ending the war.

Operation Downfall

What if President Truman had decided not to use the A-bomb? Or, what if the two A-bombs that he authorized had not activated when they were dropped on Hiroshima and Nagasaki? These are obviously rhetorical questions, but it is interesting to consider what was planned and what might possibly have resulted.

Over a period of months, the Joint Chiefs of Staff in Washington, DC, had developed the grand design of plans to invade the Home Islands of Japan. The top-secret, two-phase invasion plan, *Operation Downfall,* consisted of *Olympic*, aimed at Kyushu, the southernmost of the four main islands, and *Coronet*, directed to the central plains of Honshu, with the main target being Tokyo. *Operation Downfall* was estimated to take place from June 1945 to August 1946. *Olympic* would be implemented first, to secure a base from which to launch *Coronet.*

The Joint Chiefs of Staff shared the planning document with Admiral Nimitz and General MacArthur and asked them to develop the details for each of their respective operations. Only President Truman could make the decision to implement *Operation Downfall.*

The U.S. Sixth Army medical staff estimated the casualties for the *Olympic* assault to be about 394,000, including 98,500 dead. The Navy projected 49,000 dead and 48,000 wounded. The combined total: 491,000 casualties for the Kyushu operation. The casualties for the *Coronet* invasion would be at least that many.

General George C. Marshall, Chairman of the Joint Chiefs of Staff, advised Truman that *Olympic*, the Kyushu operation, "would cost a minimum [of] one-quarter of a million casualties, and might cost as much as a million, on the American side alone, with an equal number of the enemy."[35]

In mid-June 1945, President Truman authorized *Olympic* knowing that the invasion would cost a large number of casualties. No atomic bomb had yet been tested to verify that it would work.

During the planning stage for *Operation Downfall*, General Marshall and Secretary Stimson agreed that nine atomic bombs would be used during *Olympic* and at least another six for *Coronet*.[36]

Truman put heavy reliance on the combined judgment of Admiral Nimitz and the Joint Chiefs of Staff; the latter told the president to expect 60,000 to 80,000 American casualties and more than a million Japanese fatalities from the planned invasion of the Japanese homelands in 1945 or 1946. Nimitz was convinced that the Americans would have to battle civilians as well as the Japanese Imperial Army and Navy.

The number of casualties in the 82-day Battle of Okinawa, running from April 1 through June 1945, was a key in helping Truman decide whether to use the atomic bomb. Okinawa was the largest sea-land-air battle in history. American casualties exceeded 38,000 wounded and 12,500 dead or missing. The island of Okinawa, just south of the four main islands of Japan, had a large indigenous civilian population. More than 100 thousand were battle casualties.

Truman reckoned that although the new device would probably kill thousands, using it to force Japan to surrender unconditionally would be the more humane route in the long run.

I, for one, think that President Truman made the right decision and, thank God, the device worked.

Superfortress on the Move

Paul Tibbets had flown 25 missions in B-17s, known as the Flying Fortress, in the European theater. In March 1943, he was returned to the States to test the combat capability of Boeing's new Superfortress, the B-29. He taught himself to fly the plane and subsequently flew it about 400 hours in tests. In September 1944, Tibbets was briefed on the Manhattan Project. He was given responsibility to organize and train a unit to deliver the atomic bomb in combat operations.

Tibbets requisitioned 15 new B-29s and specified that they be stripped of turrets and armor plating except for the tail gunner position; that fuel-injected engines and new-technology, reversible-pitch propellers be installed; and that the bomb bay be re-configured to suspend ten thousand pounds. Such an airplane would fly higher, faster, and above the effective range of anti-aircraft fire.

Tibbets organized and trained the First Ordnance Squadron to carry out the technical phases of the secret mission. Then, quietly, the group moved overseas to Tinian Island in the Marianas chain. Tibbets, by then 30 years old, was promoted to Colonel and appointed to pilot the B-29 Superfortress to carry the first atomic bomb to Japan. He named his plane the *Enola Gay*, after his mother.

On the afternoon of August 5, 1945, President Truman issued his decision to use the atomic bomb against Japan. At 2:45 a.m. on August 6, the *Enola Gay* lifted off Tinian's North Field en route to Hiroshima. At exactly 9:45 a.m. plus 15 seconds, the world's first atomic bomb was used in combat.

Oppenheimer had told Tibbets that it would be unsafe to continue on a straight path, as pilots normally did after dropping a bomb. So, Tibbets had trained himself to turn the *Enola Gay,* immediately, 159 degrees in 40 seconds, so that the plane would not get the full force of the blast at 25,000 feet. Even so, the plane was hit with 2.5 Gs of force at 10 ½ miles distance when the bomb exploded.

The untested uranium-235 bomb, nicknamed Little Boy, was airburst 1,900 feet above the city to maximize destruction. When the heat wave reached ground level, it burnt all before it, including people. Col. Tibbets reported, "We turned back to look at Hiroshima. The city was hidden by that awful cloud … boiling up, mushrooming."

The co-pilot, Robert Lewis, pounding on Tibbets's shoulder, said, "Look at that! Look at that! Look at that!" Then, he wrote in his journal, "My God, what have we done?"[37]

Two-thirds of the city of Hiroshima was destroyed. The population actually present at the time was estimated at 350,000; of these, 140,000 died by the end of the year.

There was apparently no indication yet that the Japanese leaders were willing to accept unconditional surrender.

The second weapon, a duplicate of the plutonium-239 implosion assembly tested in Trinity and nicknamed Fat Man, was carried by a B-29 named *Bock's Car* and dropped on Nagasaki at 11:02 a.m. on August 9. About half the city was destroyed. Of the estimated 270,000 people present at the time, about 70,000 died by the end of the year.[38]

Less than a week after the A-bomb was dropped on Nagasaki, the Japanese leaders indicated that they had had enough. Japan surrendered to the Allies on August 14, 1945, when Emperor Hirohito accepted the terms of the Potsdam Declaration. They would surrender unconditionally. The following day, the Emperor announced Japan's surrender on the radio. This was the first time the Japanese people had ever heard his voice; until then, he was considered a god.

In the U.S., it was V-J (Victory Japan) Day, the end of World War II. Automobile horns and factory whistles blew. Sirens wailed. Church bells rang. In Davao, we lacked the bells and whistles, but made up for it in cheers and whoopees. Doc Koch poured each of us Pill Rollers a shot of Bourbon from his medicinal supply and offered a toast: "Here's to our going home!"

After downing my shot with a Coke chaser, I went back to my pup tent, thinking of Florence, and sobbed with joy. Seven months after I had joined the outfit on Leyte, the war was over. That seven months had seemed like seven centuries.

A few days later, I had a V-mail letter from Florence:

Dearest Leon:

I am ecstatic that the war is over. The news came over the radio this morning. Fire trucks cruised Winchester with sirens wailing. The glass factory's whistle could be heard for miles. I drove Dad's 1941 Ford to join others touring the town square, blowing horns. What excitement! What joy!

Oh, honey, I cannot tell you how happy I am that you will soon be coming home. I miss you so very much, but now that I know you are safe, I will wait patiently for your return.

I love you more than you can imagine, my darling, with all my heart.

Your Sweetheart,

Florence

It would be months before I would return to the States, but the pain and fear of combat was lifted. What a relief! I could now dream of the future. I imagined that Florence was in my arms. A whole new life lay before us.

Hesser showing off at Davao Gulf, after the war ended, with Joe Lahey (top) and Oscar Musselman (middle) from Indiana

Chapter 9: Army of Occupation

My image of the Japanese had been forged largely at Camp Hood in Killers Kollege, where we were taught to "kill the damn Japs!" Experience in the Philippines indicated that the determined Japanese would fight to the last, rather than surrender. What would be their reaction to an "army of occupation"? Barely two months after Hiroshima, as I boarded a ship at Davao Gulf, part of a huge convoy destined for Japan, I was certain that the Japanese people would not roll over and play dead. Somehow, they would get back at us when we least expected it.

The night before we were to go ashore, as we harbored off the island of Shikoku, the smallest of the four main islands, I tried to visualize what to expect the next day. Though I was no longer a teenager—I had recently turned 20—I was scared. I felt an eerie sensation, undoubtedly stemming from the bloody fighting and killing on Luzon and Mindanao.

Now, when we disembarked the next morning, marching in formation through one after another of Shikoku's villages, all was silent. I saw not one person, except for an occasional four- or five-year-old child peeping wide eyed around the corner of a house, or once-in-a-while a stray dog. I thought, *When are they going to drop the other shoe?*

The other shoe never dropped.

The Japanese economy was a shambles, with widespread destruction and poverty. The homes of hundreds of thousands of Japanese had been destroyed in the B-29 bombing raids. Medical facilities and transportation networks were virtually nonexistent. Thousands of city dwellers were on the edge of starvation.

MacArthur immediately set several laws for the occupying troops. Among them: No Allied personnel were to fraternize with Japanese people. No Allied personnel were to assault Japanese people. No Allied personnel were to eat the scarce Japanese food.

Among MacArthur's first official actions was to set up a food distribution network. He sent a curt message to Washington, "Send food or send more troops." Washington responded with shiploads of wheat, rice and other foods.

After a few days on Shikoku it was evident, and went against everything we'd been taught, that the Japanese civilians were a caring, sincere, hardworking, peace-loving people. Within two weeks, we GIs were putting our arms around giggling girls and communicating through sign language. Japanese adults, mostly women and older men, were genuinely polite. If they harbored humility because of their military's defeat, it didn't show. They held their heads high, and seemed happy that the war was over.

Women whom we saw on the street wore brightly colored, though often tattered, clothes that looked strange to us Americans.

To us battle-worn soldiers, the Japanese were an enigma. We found it hard to get inside their minds. How could a people who had seemed so warlike, who had introduced the world to *kamikaze*, suddenly become so peaceful?

Until the mid-19th century, Japan's policy had been isolationist for more than two centuries. In 1852, President Millard Fillmore gave Commodore Mathew Perry the task of opening diplomatic relations with Japan. Perry sailed into Tokyo Bay in July 1853 with a "resolute attitude" and eventually, on March 31, 1854, signed the first treaty between the United States and Japan.

The treaty opened up trade and diplomatic relations, but at the time of Japan's attack on Pearl Harbor most Americans, especially those of us in the Midwest, had never even seen a Japanese person. In 1940, only 29 people of Japanese descent resided in the entire state of Indiana.[39]

At Lincoln High, in the heartland of America, we had become aware of and studied our European heritage. But, virtually no time was given to the study of the Japanese and their way of life—they were the enemy; that's all we needed to know.

Exploring the Cities

Shikoku, which literally means "four lands," lies to the south of Honshu and northeast of Kyushu. It is a rural backwater with fewer attractions than exist on the main island of Honshu. The land is primarily agricultural, known especially for its citrus groves.

Economically, the island was flat on its back. Few personal vehicles were running. Gasoline was nearly nonexistent, since our submarines had torpedoed most of the ships carrying oil to Japan.

Mysteriously to us Americans, fuel for the few trucks that were running was from charcoal. About an hour before a truck was to make a delivery, the driver would start a charcoal fire in a burner on the rear of the truck. Gas from the charcoal, captured in a hood over the burner, went through a pipe to the engine. When enough gas accumulated, the driver would start the engine and proceed—slowly—on his journey. He would stop periodically to stoke the charcoal. There was no road rage or honking of horns.

As one who was raised on a farm, I was especially interested in the "honey buckets" in the corner of nearly every farm field. This was organic farming at its best. A honey bucket was simply a large hole that was dug in the corner of a field into which all kinds of waste materials were stored: animal manure, human feces, green foliage and agricultural wastes. After the materials fermented, they were spread by hand on the field to serve as fertilizer for the next crop. The results were spectacular, if odiferous.

During my short time on Shikoku, I "explored" a few of its cities. One of Shikoku's largest cities, Takamatsu, seemed mostly devoid of commerce. But as is the case throughout Japan, the city did have a number of parks with exquisite gardens and pedestrian bridges that arched over beautifully landscaped ponds. I was fascinated by the contrast between the drab commercial areas and the glorious parks.

One of Japan's many fabulous parks, 1945

Just outside the city of Matsuyama is Japan's oldest and much-revered Dogo Onsen hot spring. An adjoining three-story public bathhouse, built in the late 19th century, was popular with the local residents. At this early stage of the Occupation, we GIs were advised

not to take part in the luxury, since we would likely be neither welcomed nor comfortable in the coeducational facility.

The routine for our 34th Regiment was to move every few weeks to a different city, to show our presence as part of the Occupation forces. After a short time on Shikoku, we crossed over to the main island of Honshu where, in turn, we "occupied" Kure, Kobe, Osaka, and Kyoto during the time that I was in Japan.

While at Kure, a group of us GIs took a Jeep a short distance to what had been the city of Hiroshima. Even though we had been told what to expect, I was aghast as we approached the site. For several square miles, all was rubble with an occasional standing pillar. The entire city had evaporated. Pungent odors saturated the air. Although it was only slightly more than two months since the A-bomb had been dropped, no one suggested that we should worry about radiation.

Except for a young man who was selling pictures that had been taken of the area just days after August 6, no Japanese were in sight. I bought a set of sixteen of the pictures, on the back of which were short descriptions in Japanese of what the photos represented. Later, I had the Japanese statements translated to English. I still have the pictures.

Hiroshima

At each post, our job in the 2nd Battalion aid station was to find appropriate quarters and arrange to hold sick call. By that time, I had been promoted to Staff Sergeant with responsibility for organizing the routine: making a roster of the staff, showing who was to be on duty each day, and assuring that we had sufficient supplies. Several of the old-timers of the cadre of Pill Rollers had gone back to the States to be discharged, so we had a much smaller staff than we had during battle. Even so, the duty was light and we had lots of free time. Several times each week, a few of us would go into whatever city we were next to and scout around.

On one of those excursions, I went into a jewelry store to see about getting my Longines watch fixed. I had taken the second hand off when it lodged and stopped the timepiece while I was in the Philippines. The jeweler, an elderly man, understood through sign language what the problem was and how grateful I would be to get it fixed. He readily agreed and in a few days had crafted a new second hand that made it fully functional again. I paid him with a carton of cigarettes and some candy, which seemed to make him as happy as I was to have the watch repaired.

At our next post, near Kobe City, we Pill Rollers became friends with two Japanese boys; we called them Mutt and Jeff. They cheerfully helped us clean the aid station, prepared "hotsy mesu," or boiling water, when asked and generally did whatever small tasks we gave them. We were not exploiting them; they were grateful for the candy and other favors that we gave them.

Hesser with Mutt and Jeff

One day, the Major who was the Battalion commander dropped in the aid station, unannounced, for an inspection. When he entered the door, he saw Mutt sitting on a chair, looking through one of the magazines from our tea table. I can still visualize and hear the Major's shriek and animated gestures. He shouted, "Mother of Christ, what's going on here!" We were breaking the rule: Thou shalt not fraternize with the Japanese. Mutt stood up, I turned and kicked him in the butt and motioned for him to get out of there. That apparently satisfied the Major, who promptly left. When the Major was out of sight, I motioned for Mutt to come back in and we laughed our heads off.

The Japanese hot baths became a favorite of us dogfaces. Each small community had a bathhouse with a large tub, like a small swimming pool, with very hot water. Traditionally, after removing their clothing in separate rooms, the men, women and children of the community all lounged in the bath at the same time. MacArthur's staff was a bit concerned that we GIs would have a hard time adjusting to that custom, so they arranged for separate bath houses for the Allied troops.

Of all the cities that our 34th Regiment occupied, Osaka, Japan's third largest city and a major port, was the most interesting to me. Among its attractions was the magnificent Osaka Castle, which dates from the 16th century. It occupies about one square kilometer of land. From the outside, it appears to be five stories. On the inside, it has eight stories. Surrounded by moats, it is built on top of a tall stone foundation to protect its occupants from sword-bearing attackers. Unfortunately, the main tower was damaged by bombing raids in 1945. It has since been renovated.

I found Osaka's Kaiyukan Aquarium, one of the largest in the world, truly fascinating. Some of its tanks stretch over several floors. Among other sea-life creatures, one tank housed a large whale shark. Osaka also has many Buddhist temples, shrines, amusement parks and museums, some of which I had time to visit.

Kyoto, where we were stationed just before I was to return to the States, was Japan's capital and the residence of the Emperor from 794 until 1868. With its hundreds of Buddhist temples, its raked-pebble gardens and mysterious Shinto shrines, it was the cultural center of Japan. Americans dropped leaflets on Kyoto during the war, telling the people that we were not against the Japanese people and their culture and due to its historical value, the city would not be bombed. Kyoto was not chosen as a target of air raids during the war. The Japanese were grateful.

Throughout the country, Japan's trains were overcrowded, sweaty and smelly, like scenes from a movie out of Bombay, India. Men rode on top of passenger cars or hung on the rear or sides. It was common, and fascinating to us Americans, to see a train slowly proceed through town as a man stood on the packed stairway of an overflowing passenger car, leaning forward, steadying himself with one arm attached to a stabilizing bar at the entrance, and relieving himself. When you gotta go, you gotta go.

Establishing Postwar Policies

General Douglas MacArthur deserves much credit for Japan's smooth transition from a war mentality to a peaceful environment. On August 15, the day after V-J Day, President Truman appointed MacArthur as Supreme Commander of the Allied Powers (SCAP), to supervise the occupation of Japan. The General arrived in Tokyo on August 30. In Tokyo Bay, aboard Admiral Nimitz' flagship the USS *Missouri* on September 2, 1945, MacArthur along with representatives of our Allies accepted the surrender.

I suspect, but cannot confirm, that MacArthur himself planned a stunning show of force for the occasion; 426 B-29s flew at 1,000 feet altitude over the battleship *Missouri* as he signed the surrender documents. The performance included 42 groups of eleven planes. Each group was led by three planes in inverted V formation. Behind each leg of the V were four planes flying in a diamond formation. It must have been spectacular.[40]

The Allies had developed a list of war criminals, of people to be tried in a court tribunal in Tokyo. Emperor Hirohito—the person who was deemed ultimately responsible—was at the top of the list. MacArthur's staff advised that he should abolish the office of the emperor and make it clear that he, General MacArthur, was in charge.

MacArthur had a thorough knowledge of Japan and its culture; he understood their customs and mores. He had first spent time in Japan as a 25-year-old in 1909 to work with his father, General Arthur MacArthur, who was Military Attaché to the U.S. Embassy in Tokyo. Douglas understood well the importance of the Emperor to the Japanese people. He had no problem with trying the generals and admirals on the war criminals list, but he hesitated about the Emperor.

MacArthur decided to meet with the Emperor to try to win his support. He made it known that he would welcome a visit from the Emperor, but would not go to him. The Emperor agreed. On September 28, he went to the American Embassy for an informal visit. Except for an interpreter selected by the Emperor, as suggested by MacArthur, no others were present. Following cordial greetings, Emperor Hirohito said, "General, I want you to know, that I, as emperor, am responsible for everything that occurred in the war. And you must do what you feel you must do."[41]

MacArthur was kind and courteous and did not insult the Emperor. He was impressed with Hirohito's attitude. Following the meeting, he gave it more thought and decided that the Emperor could play a helpful role in the reconstruction of Japan and in calming the Japanese people. He announced to the Joint Chiefs of Staff that the Emperor's name should be removed from the war criminals list.

There was never any doubt about General MacArthur's authority as Supreme Commander; the Joint Chiefs of Staff had sent him a message saying, "Your authority is absolute ..." Even so, he preferred to work through the existing bureaucracy, implemented as a civilian, not a military, government. The Emperor, as a symbol of continuity and cohesion of the Japanese people, could be helpful.

The Potsdam Declaration had outlined some basic reforms to be instituted following the Japanese surrender: Destroy their weapons. Replace the imperial form of government with a democracy. Give women equal rights. Give feudal farmers an opportunity to own land. MacArthur was in full agreement with each of the objectives. The question was how best to accomplish them.

A new constitution was a prerequisite. A committee of scholars and government people was appointed to write a new constitution. When the group did not come up with anything acceptable—they apparently didn't understand the principles of a constitution based on democracy—MacArthur said, "Okay, let's write a constitution based on the principles of the American Constitution."[42]

With the help of some sharp lawyers, a constitution was developed. MacArthur worked it over a bit and then gave it to the Japanese cabinet, saying, "I would like your concurrence with this, but if you don't concur I'll probably do it anyway."[43]

The cabinet didn't know what to do, so they sent it to the Emperor. In a few days the Emperor said, "I like it. This is the way Japan should go."[44]

With that, the cabinet put it before the people in a referendum. It was overwhelmingly approved.

With the sanction of Japan's reigning monarch, MacArthur began the detailed work of the Occupation. Among the accomplishments by the time the Occupation ended officially on April 28, 1952, were:

- Disarmament: Japan's new constitution banned Japan from maintaining armed forces;
- Liberalization: In a major land reform, five million acres were taken from landlords and given to the farmers who

worked them;

- Women were Franchised: Women voted in 1946 for the first time;
- War Leaders were Purged: Military tribunals tried Japan's war criminals and sentenced many to death and imprisonment.

The Occupation left a lasting impact. Democracy, freedom of the press, and rejection of militarism and nationalism are legacies of General Douglas MacArthur's post-war policies. Japan quickly achieved spectacular growth, to become the second largest economy in the world. Ironically, there was more resentment by some politicians in Washington, DC, than existed among the Japanese people for General MacArthur's power and what he was doing.

Among those tried as war criminals was General Hideki Tojo, who as Prime Minister at the time had ordered the bombing of Pearl Harbor. For awhile in Japan, Tojo grew in confidence and popularity. He began to style himself in the manner of a Fascist leader. However, following a series of military disasters, culminating in the fall of Saipan, he was forced to resign on July 18, 1944. After the war, Tojo was tried for war crimes by the International Military Tribunal for the Far East. He was sentenced to death on November 12, 1948 and executed by hanging on December 23, 1948.

Final Tour of Duty

We Pill Rollers had a fairly relaxed tour of duty in Japan. It was rare for any of the troops to show up for morning sick call. We would occasionally give penicillin shots to those GIs who were afraid they might have been "exposed." They would come into the aid station and say something like, "I'm due to rotate back to the States next month, Sarg; how about a round of penicillin, just to kinda clean up my blood?" We generally obliged.

As the time approached for me to return to the States to be discharged, I contemplated what I might take as a gift for Florence, my fiancé. I finally decided to have some undies—panties and bra—tailor-made from pure silk fabric. Silk was practically nonexistent in the States during the war. This would be something she would cherish and perhaps wear at our wedding.

What size should they be? I closed my eyes and tried to visualize Florence. I had never seen her undressed.

With the aid of sign language and the help of an attractive and shapely Japanese sales girl, we estimated the sizes. She showed me a sample bra. Having observed that Japanese girls were generally flat-chested, I gestured, "No, not that size. Bigger."

In response to her suggested panties, I signaled, "Smaller."

After we agreed on sizes, she pointed to a calendar to convey, "Okay. They'll be ready in a week."

On the designated day, I picked up the undies and, longingly, packed them in my duffle bag. I couldn't wait to return to the States and embrace my sweetheart.

My imagination was running wild. I would soon see my fiancé model her new lingerie.

Chapter 10: Discharge and Welcome Home

Finally, the day came for me to board ship and sail for Seattle. In the Army's inimitable fashion, the night before we were to board, all Staff Sergeants—fifteen of us—were bunked in the same room at our military facilities at the Port of Yokohama. Next morning, the face of one of the fellas was broken out with an obvious case of chicken pox. What should he do? A few of us urged that he cover his face as best he could and proceed to board ship. The majority, sensibly, argued that he should report to sick call. The result: All fifteen of us were summarily quarantined for three weeks.

One of the mathematical geniuses in the group calculated that if each of us came down consecutively with the malady, we would be in quarantine for three and a half years. Fortunately, none did. We boarded another ship at the end of the three-week hiatus. Compared with the troop carriers that we were accustomed to, the cruise was not too bad. The Navy chow was much better than our routine Army meals. Perhaps much of the perceived improvement was because I was headed home rather than to war.

I volunteered to serve on the night shift as a medic, which meant that I was assigned a comfortable bed in the ship's hospital during the day. About the only action I saw as a medic on the return trip was to administer some shots, including to one of the nurses, to whom I gave injections of penicillin. I didn't ask why she needed them.

When we reached Seattle after nine days at sea, I felt like kissing the ground as I walked off the gang plank. America the beautiful! To top it off, local ladies lined up to serve each of us a glass of fresh milk, the first we had had for nearly two years, and the best homemade oatmeal cookies I have ever eaten; I can still sense their taste and sweet smell.

As soon as I could get to a pay phone, I called Florence: "Operator, give me Winchester, Indiana, number Blue 445." That was before area codes and direct dialing. When she answered, we both cried with joy. When I quit sobbing, I explained why we had had a three-week delay. I finished the conversation by saying, "Sweetheart, I'll be home in ten days."

The train ride from Seattle to Fort Benjamin Harrison in Indianapolis was much more pleasant than the one that I had taken from Richmond, Indiana to Camp Stoneman, California in 1944. The wild flowers of June and other foliage in Oregon and onward were magnificent. Fellow passengers were kind and courteous. I only wished that the train would go faster.

Finally, we arrived at Fort Ben. I was offered a bonus to reenlist. I said, "Thanks, but no thanks; I have other plans. I'm going to get married and start a family."

From Fort Ben, after I was officially discharged on June 10, 1946, I took a two-hour bus ride to Winchester. The town's bus station was about six blocks from the Life family's residence at 407 High Street. I ran all the way. Though my barracks bag contained all of my earthly possessions, it had never felt lighter; it slowed me only slightly.

Elderly Mrs. Mamie Davis, across the street from the Life family, called Florence and said, "There's a soldier running up the street carrying a duffle bag. Is he yours?"

Life Family Residence, 407 High Street

Florence met me at the door as I jogged breathlessly up to the pillared front porch. We embraced passionately, oblivious to neighbors who undoubtedly were keen observers. Once inside, Mrs. Life gave me a quick snack of milk and a generous piece of homemade chocolate cake. Then, Florence reminded me that my parents were anxiously waiting at the farm, we should go immediately. She drove me to the farm in her parents' 1941 Ford. Not only were my mother, dad and sister waiting. The driveway was filled with the cars of relatives.

Grandma Ida ran toward me with a handful of wildflowers and gave me a big hug. I introduced Florence to half a dozen aunts and uncles and countless cousins.

Then, Mother invited us all to the kitchen table to partake, cafeteria style, of one of my favorite meals: sugar-cured ham, which smelled as good as it tasted, that she and Dad had processed from pigs that they had butchered themselves. For dessert, Mother served one of her specialties: butterscotch pie topped with real whipped cream, fresh from our Brown Swiss cows.

After lunch, with pride I pulled a wad of $20 bills—my mustering out pay—from my pants pocket and counted out loud. Three hundred dollars! That was the most money I had ever handled at one time.

Later in the day, after the aunts, uncles, cousins and grandparents had left, Florence and I went upstairs to my room where I slowly unpacked my duffle bag and began putting things away. During the process, I retrieved the package that contained the hand-made silk lingerie that I had had tailored in Japan. With a burst of excitement, I handed Florence the package and said, "This is something that I had especially made for you in Japan. I thought you might want to wear them in our wedding."

Her face flushed when she opened the package. She said, "Oh, Honey, thank you so very much. They are absolutely beautiful—and hand-embroidered! But, Sweetheart, ..." Then she burst into laughter: the white silk panties were way too tiny and the hand-embroidered rose-colored bra was large enough for Jane Russell or Dolly Parton.

I spent two or three days visiting neighbors and friends, mostly in company with Florence in Dad's 1939 Ford. Other neighbors came to the Hesser farmstead to welcome me home. I was treated like a hero, as if I had won the war all by myself.

During precious moments alone together, Florence told me how lonely, even depressed, she had been during recent months. Until then, she spent much time with three other young women, whose husbands were also overseas. The girls went to movies or church together. They shared feelings. The three husbands, who were older than I, had been away for nearly four years and, as a consequence, were discharged earlier. Those three couples then had their own lives. Florence was alone. And lonely. The three-week delay in my leaving Japan due to chickenpox had compounded the situation.

But now, the storm clouds had lifted. The sun shone brightly. Life was glorious, like a series of rainbows. We could dream about and plan our future.

I went to the county courthouse in Winchester to register my discharge. I knew well the Randolph County Recorder, Merritt Monks, who had been a prominent referee of high school baseball and basketball games when I was playing. Merritt said, "Leon, while you're here, why don't you register to vote?"

I said, "Merritt, I'm not old enough yet to vote."

In a thundering voice that could be heard all over the courthouse, Merritt said, "Now isn't *that* a Hell of a note—been away for two years fighting in the war and still not old enough to vote!"

I also went to see Reed Abel, owner of the Ford agency in town. While I was in Japan, at my request, Dad had put my name in with Mr. Abel for a new 1946 Ford. New cars were still in short supply. Reed said, "I have put your name pretty high on the list for a new car. Unfortunately, with all the backorders, it will be a few months before it comes in."

I had been home only a few days when my mother asked me a question, when we were alone, that I am certain had weighed heavily on her mind: "Did you have to kill anyone, Son?"

Thank goodness I could say, truthfully, "No, Mother, I never fired a shot."

Then, I added, "Well, I did shoot at a stray rooster once. I missed him." We both laughed.

Following a bit of small talk, Mother said, "You're not going to get married right away, are you?"

With a straight face, I said, "No, of course not. We're going to wait until I'm 21." That would be in July, the next month.

Seeing that it was inevitable, and perhaps to secure a few more days at home for her hero son, Mother suggested that the wedding be on her birthday, Sunday, August 11. Florence thought that was a great idea. She planned a late-afternoon wedding to be held in Winchester's United Methodist Church.

Sunday, August 11 turned out to be the hottest day of the year in Winchester, Indiana. The church was packed with friends and family from both sides. And that was before the church was air-conditioned. Florence had been to a friend's wedding several days earlier in which guests continued to arrive after the ceremony had started. That would not happen in *her* wedding. She indicated in the invitations that the wedding would be at 6:00 p.m., but actually delayed the ceremony until 30 minutes later. Everyone was on time according to the invitation, which meant that they sweltered in the heat for 30 minutes before the ceremony started. Meanwhile, some wondered whether I might have had second thoughts.

The Bride and Groom

Other than that it was a beautiful wedding. Florence asked my sister, Vivian, to be maid of honor and three close friends to be bridesmaids. My good friend Wayne McGuire was best man and two cousins and a schoolmate were groomsmen. Florence's brother, Hugh Jacob, played an inspiring violin rendition of *Ave Maria*. Florence's friend, Betty Sue, sang *The Lord's Prayer* and *I Love You Truly*. Reverend Boase officiated as the vows were exchanged. I was in seventh heaven as I lifted the veil and kissed my beautiful and bubbly wife.

We retired to the church parlor for the reception and cut the cake as the bridesmaids served the guests. The Hesser and Life families and friends mingled and became better acquainted as Florence and I unwrapped and recorded the names of givers of more than two hundred gifts. All-in-all, it was a fabulous wedding—the highlight of the year in the small town of Winchester, Indiana.

After the reception, we drove Dad's 1939 Ford to Fort Wayne, about 65 miles north of Winchester, where we spent a blissful night in the honeymoon suite at the Indiana Hotel. Before I awakened the next morning, Florence slipped out of bed and went to the bathroom to freshen up and put on new makeup. Then, she slipped quietly back in bed. When I awakened, I said, "Oh, Honey, you are just as beautiful in the morning as you are when you go to bed." Much later, she told me her little secret.

We took a week for the honeymoon. Following two days in Detroit, where we stayed at the Betsy Ross Inn and toured Greenfield Village, we enjoyed three days in Canada on the way to Niagara Falls, our main destination.

At Niagara, I was inspired by the serenity of the sights and sounds as the water gracefully floated over the Falls, in contrast with the gruesome sights and sounds that I had witnessed in the Philippines and, later, at Hiroshima.

After two wonderful days at the falls, we had only one day to drive back to Indiana in time to go to work. Florence still had her job in the personnel office at the local glass factory. Father Life had arranged for me to start a job on Monday morning as an apprentice toolmaker at Kelly Tool Company. The pay was 60 cents an hour plus a $90 monthly stipend based on the GI-Bill, a provision passed by Congress that allowed veterans' wages to be supplemented while they learned a vocation or worked as an apprentice. (After a few months, the job became too confining for me. Florence lovingly agreed to become a farmer's wife.)

At $60 a month, a cozy three-room apartment awaited us on our return to Winchester from the honeymoon. In those days, we never locked the house; in this small, Midwestern town, burglaries almost never occurred. But on one of our first nights in the apartment, we were abruptly awakened when all the lights suddenly came on. Twenty friends from our Rural Youth group, including my sister Vivian, had slipped into our living room to *bell* us, a local tradition that was doted on newlyweds. As part of the tradition, Florence and

I were transported in a farm trailer, complete with bales of straw for seats, behind one of the convoy of cars that circled the town's square with horns blowing. Then, we were hauled five miles to a farm home for a newlywed party.

Some in the group asked us how we had enjoyed the fabulous lighting on Niagara Falls at night. Sheepishly, I had to say, "We didn't see the lighting at the Falls; they didn't turn the lights on until 9 o'clock."

A few weeks after we returned from our honeymoon, Mr. Abel phoned me to say, "We just got in a new four-door, black, Super DeLuxe Ford. Would you be interested?" I was. Using money that Uncle Sam had deposited in my postal savings account while I was overseas, I paid cash. The sticker price: $1,392.

From the day of the wedding, Mrs. Life, who had had higher expectations for a son-in-law than a farm boy, was definitely on my side. She was a wonderful mother-in-law. I could do no wrong.

# # #

Epilogue

Shortly after Florence and I were married, I embarked on a farming career in response to the adage: *You can take the boy off the farm, but you can't take the farm out of the boy.* We had two lovely children: first a daughter, Gwendolyn Ann, and then a son, George Christian. We made friends with other young neighboring farm families in the rural Indiana community. But, something was missing.

Gwendolyn and George

Florence knew that I regretted that I had not gone to college. One day when I came in for lunch, on my plate was a magazine article that described a young couple in their late 20s, with two children, in which the husband was a freshman at the University of Georgia. Florence said, "If he can do it, you can too." That was a life-altering moment.

At age 30, I sold the farm business and entered Purdue University as a freshman. It was so much easier than farming that I stayed on and earned a Ph.D. in Agricultural Economics.

When I was halfway through my Master's degree, the professors were saying, "Hesser, you should stay on and get a Ph.D." Florence also encouraged me. She said, "You must get your doctor's degree."

I said, "Florence, I will not go beyond the Master's degree

unless you quit your job as a secretary and study at the university."

We had that discussion a dozen or more times, always ending up with her saying, "No, it isn't necessary for me to go to school. I'll continue working. You go ahead."

One day we were on a picnic and the subject came up again. She said, "Leon, you must get your Ph.D."

Once again, I said, "Florence, I will *not* go beyond the Master's degree unless you go to school."

She hesitated, hung her head, and said, "I don't think I'm smart enough."

In a knee-jerk reaction, I said, "You are right. You are not smart enough!"

The reverse psychology worked. The next month, at age 35, Florence was a freshman in Purdue's School of Science and Humanities. She received her BA degree in the same ceremony in which I received the Ph.D.

We then went to Kansas City where I worked for three years in the Research Department of the Federal Reserve Bank. Florence taught school and went to college at night to earn a Master's degree in Reading Education.

Shortly afterward, in 1966, I joined the Foreign Service. We were posted in Pakistan where I served as director of America's technical assistance to help increase food production. Both India and Pakistan suffered widespread hunger with pockets of starvation. Two provinces in northeast India were in famine conditions. Though the U.S., Australia and Canada had been sending millions of tons of food grains each year for the past few years, the situation was getting worse.

Two widely-read books were written in the mid-1960s that, in effect, said, *Let's give up on India and Pakistan. It's hopeless. Let them die off. Let's provide our food aid to countries that have a chance.*[45]

That was the sentiment when Dr. Norman Borlaug, a Rockefeller Foundation agricultural scientist, came to the rescue. He briefed me on the high-yielding varieties of wheat that he and his colleagues had developed that relieved hunger in Mexico and said, "Based on preliminary field trials in India and Pakistan, I think they will work here as well." I jumped at the chance to help introduce the new wheat varieties and associated technology.

The American Ambassador approved my grant proposal to

import 50 tons of Borlaug's wheat seeds from Mexico. The twelve American agricultural advisors on my team worked with members of Pakistan's agricultural extension service who, in turn, introduced the new technology to the country's farmers. Within four years, wheat yields in Pakistan doubled to 8 million tons per year. It took a bit longer in India, but both countries were then self-sufficient in food grains and no longer needed to depend on food aid. To be a part of what was called "The Green Revolution" was indeed gratifying. In 1970, Norman Borlaug was awarded the Nobel Peace Prize for saving millions of lives from starvation. Now in his mid-90s and still quite alert and active, Norman and I remain close friends.

During the 1970s, I was transferred to State Department headquarters in Washington, DC, where I served as director of the U.S. Government's worldwide program to help increase food production in less developed countries. My office of agriculture had five divisions— crops, livestock, economics, soil and water, and fisheries—and a $50 million per year budget. Being responsible for that operation, and seeing the positive results throughout Asia, Africa, and Latin America, was a rewarding counterbalance to the death and destruction that I had witnessed as a soldier at ZigZag Pass.

Without doubt, the time in the Philippines and Japan during and immediately after World War II inspired me to want to see more of the world and to try to level the playing field. My playing a role in extending life-giving benefits—relieving hunger and poverty of the world's poorer people—has indeed been healing.

Florence earns a Doctor's Degree at Ball State University

When we returned to the States from Pakistan, Florence earned an Ed.D. at Ball State University and became Professor and Director of the Reading Center at George Washington University, where she served for twenty years. During the four years that the Carters were in Washington, Amy Carter was in the Center's after-school program. Florence had several parent conferences in the White House, some in the Oval Office where the President and Mrs. Carter made her feel welcomed and at ease.

At the request of Princess Haifa, daughter of King Faisal and wife of Saudi Arabia's Ambassador to Washington, Florence and her staff interviewed, selected and trained for two years twenty Saudis—ten women and ten men—who returned to Jeddah and replicated Florence's Reading Center.

Our having gone from young Indiana tenant farmers to the world stage and on to the pinnacles of power in Washington was more than we could have imagined on the night that Florence and I parked beside Fudge's gravel pit and embraced, the night before I left Winchester to go overseas as a teenage soldier.

Though I have now logged more than a million miles in the air, the trip from Yokohama to Seattle in 1946 was my last ocean voyage. Florence is suggesting that we should take a Mediterranean cruise in August 2010, to celebrate our 64th wedding anniversary. She assures me that on a luxury cruise ship, unlike troopships, one does not have to stand up to eat his meals. Sounds like a great plan.

Appendix A: U.S. Army Ranks during World War II

Officers

General	Four stars
Lieutenant General	Three stars
Major General	Two stars
Brigadier General	One star
Colonel	Silver eagle
Lieutenant Colonel	Silver leaf
Major	Gold leaf
Captain	Two silver bars
1st Lieutenant	One silver bar
2nd Lieutenant	One gold bar

Non-Commissioned Officers

First Sergeant	Three stripes above, three below
Master Sergeant	Three stripes above, two below
Staff Sergeant	Three stripes above, one below
Sergeant	Three stripes
Corporal	Two stripes

Enlisted Personnel

| Private First Class | One stripe |
| Private | |

Appendix B: Army Unit Sizes

Unit	Approximate Personnel	Composition
Army	100,000	2+ corps, HQ
Corps	30,000+	2+ divisions
Division	15,000+	3 brigades, HQ, support units
Brigade	4,500+	3+ regiments, HQ
Regiment	1,500+	2+ battalions, HQ
Battalion	700	4+ companies, HQ
Company	175	4 platoons, HQ
Platoon	40	4 squads
Squad	10	

Bibliography

Bradley, James. *Flags of Our Fathers.* New York: Bantam, 2000.

Dear, I.C.B., General Editor. *The Oxford Companion to World War II.* New York: Oxford University Press, 1995.

Goldstein, Donald M., et al. *Rain of Ruin: Photographic History of Hiroshima & Nagasaki.* Dulles, Virginia: Brassey's, 1995.

Hartman, Doris. *My Life in Hiroshima, 1952-1981.* Three Rivers, Massachusetts: Van Volumes, 2000.

Hersey, John. *Hiroshima.* New York: A.A. Knopf, 1985 (hardcover); Vintage Books, 1989 (paperback).

Hesser, Leon. *Nurture the Heart, Feed the World.* Austin: Synergy Books, 2004.

Hornfischer, James D. *The Last Stand of the Tin Can Sailors.* New York: Bantam, 2004.

MacArthur, Brian. *Surviving the Sword: Prisoners of the Japanese in the Far East, 1942-45.* New York: Random House, 2005.

Mann, David B. *Avenging Bataan: The Battle of ZigZag Pass.* Raleigh: Portland Press, 2001.

North, Oliver. *War Stories II: Heroism in the Pacific.* Washington, DC: Regnery Publishing, 2004.

Reynolds, Norman. *X-Day.* West Conshohocken, PA: Infinity Publishing, 2006.

Shohei, Ooka. *Taken Captive: A Japanese POW's Story.* John Wiley & Sons, Inc. (Originally published in 1952. English language translation copyright, 1996)

Stodghill, Dick. *Normandy 1944: A Young Rifleman's War.* Baltimore: Publish America, 2006.

Takiff, Michael. *Brave Men, Gentle Heros: American Fathers and Sons in World War II and Vietnam.* Harper Collins, 2003.

Valtin, Jan. *Children of Yesterday: The Twenty-Fourth Infantry Division in World War II.* Nashville, Battery Press, 1988.

Wahle, Benjamin. "The Men of Company 'G' 34th Infantry," *Taro Leaf,* Vol. 59, No. 3, Summer 2005.

Webb, James. *The Emperor's General.* New York: Bantam, 2000.

Index

A
A-bomb, 82-86, 88
"American ugly ducklings," 35
Anti-Tank Training, 30
Army of Occupation, 91-101
Atabrine, a substitute for quinine, 69, 79
Austin, 1st Lt. Paul, 43-44
Australia, 16, 38
Avenging Bataan, David Mann, 58
B
B-17 Flying Fortress, 38, 57
B-25 Mitchell bomber, 20
B-29 Superfortress, 71, 85, 87-88, 98
Bagobos, 75
BAR (Browning Automatic .30 caliber rifle), 52, 62, 67, 76
Barracks #175, 25-26, 30-31
Bataan, Bataan Peninsula, 16, 39, 51, 53
Bataan Death March, 16, 37, 39
Battle of the Bulge, World War II, 9
Benjamin Harrison, Fort, 24-25, 103-104
"Betty Bomber," Japanese heavy bomber, also known as "Flying Cigar" and "One-Shot Lighter," 47
Biak, 48
Bock's Car, 88
Bonsai, 77
Borlaug, Norman, 11, 112-113
Borneo, 37
Breakneck Ridge, 44-45
C
Cameron, Capt., Surgeon, 2nd BN, 34th Regiment, 58, 63-64
Camp Hood, Texas, 5, 10, 25-31, 41, 59, 76, 80, 91
Camp Stoneman, California, 33, 103
Caribou Gulch, 76
Carter, President and Mrs., 114
Chiang Kai-Shek, 82
China, 82-83
China-Burma-India theatre, World War II, 9

Churchill, Prime Minister Winston, 81-82
Ciancarlo, Guiseppe, 61
Clark Field, 15
Combat Infantry Badge, 67
Combat Medic Badge, 67
Coronet, 86-87
Corregidor, 39, 51
Curtis Helldiver, Navy dive bomber, 75
D
Davao City, 73-74, 77, 89
Davao Gulf, 73, 76-77, 91
Davao Province, 16, 73, 75, 82
Davy Jones initiation, 36
Dinalupihan, 50-55, 63
Dogo Onsen hot spring, 93
Doolittle, Jimmy, 20
Doolittle's Raid, 20, 41
E
Einstein, Albert, 85
Eisenberg, Morton, 42
Enola Gay, 88
F
"Fat Man" A-bomb, 88
First Ordnance Squadron, 88
Flying Tigers, 9
Foreign Service of the United States, 11, 112-113
Formosa, 41
France, 13
G
G Company, 34th Infantry Regiment, 44-46, 49, 55-65
German U-boats, 13
Germany, 13
Grapes of Wrath, The, 13
Great Depression, The, 13, 16-17
Green Revolution, The, 11, 113
Groves, Leslie R., 85
Guam, 15
Guise, Lester, 27, 31

H

I

J

Notes

1 *U.S. News and World Report*, January 30-February 6, 2006, page 52.
2 Transcription by Michael E. Eidenmuller, AmericanRhetoric.com
3 Reynolds, *X-Day*, page 401
4 Camp Hood opened officially in September 1942, named in honor of famous Confederate General John Bell Hood, an outstanding leader who gained recognition during the Civil War as the commander of Hood's Texas Brigade. In 1950, the "temporary camp" was designated Fort Hood and given permanent status as one of the largest military installations in the world.
5 Stanley is a fictitious name; I no longer remember their last name.
6 Mann, page 41
7 Eisenberg, personal diary (with permission)
8 North, page 298
9 North, pages 298 and 299
10 For a compelling account of a related battle in the Philippine Sea, October 25-27, 1944, see Hornfischer's *The Last Stand of the Tin Can Sailors*
11 24th Division History, page 37; reprinted in Summer 2005 edition of *Taro Leaf.*
12 Mann, page 43
13 Mann, page 48
14 Historical Record of the 34th Inf. Reg., reprinted in Valtin, page 313.
15 Valtin, pages 316 and 317
16 Mann, page 127
17 Mann, page 128
18 Mann, page 66
19 Mann, page 157
20 Mann, page 158
21 Mann, pages 156 and 157
22 Mann, page 112
23 Mann, page 168
24 Valtin, pages 325-326
25 Mann, page 171
26 Mann, page 178
27 Mann, page 192
28 Mann, page 178

29 Valtin, page 377
30 Valtin, pages 386-387
31 Valtin, page 358
32 Potsdam Declaration, Wikipedia
33 Dear, pages 69 to 75
34 Information on developing the first atomic bombs is abstracted from various articles of *Britannica Encyclopedia*, fifteenth edition.
35 Reynolds, page 407
36 Reynolds, page 394
37 Reported on the Internet
38 Abstracted from an article, "The Technology of War" in fifteenth edition of *Britannica Encyclopedia*
39 "Japanese Americans from Internment to Indiana," *Indiana Magazine of History*, Vol. 102, June 2006.
40 Takiff, page 25
41 North, page 415
42 North, page 416
43 North, page 416
44 North, page 416
45 Paul Ehrlich's *The Population Bomb* and *Famine 1975*, by the Paddock brothers.

Leon Hesser

Quick Order Form

Fax orders: 239-234-6198. Send this form.
Telephone orders: 239-254-1478. Have your credit card ready.
Email orders: orders@BavenderHouse.com
Postal orders: Bavender House Press, P.O. Box 770883
Naples, FL 34107-0883, USA.

Please send the following books. I understand that I may return any of them for a full refund—for any reason, no questions asked.

	Price	Number
ZigZag Pass (hardcover)	$19.95	
The Man Who Fed the World (hardcover)	$24.95	
The Man Who Fed the World (trade paperback)	$15.95	
Nurture the Heart, Feed the World (hardcover)	$14.95	
The Taming of the Wilderness (hardcover)	$26.50	
The Taming of the Wilderness (trade paperback)	$16.50	

Name: _____

Address: _____

City:_____ State:_____ Zip:_____

Telephone: _____

Email address: _____

Sales tax: Please add 6% for products shipped to Florida addresses.

No charge for shipping by Media Mail within U.S.

International, by air: $9:00 for the first book; $5:00 for each additional book.